THE NEW ZEPBOUND FOOD
BIBLE FOR BEGINNERS

Your Step-by-Step Nutrition Blueprint for Zepbound--
Lose Weight, Balance Blood Sugar, and Stay Full with
the Right Foods

DR. EDWIN MALIK

CONTENTS

Chapter 7: Juices and Sips for Hydration and Blood Sugar Balance

- Low-Sugar Vegetable Juices

- Herbal Teas and Infused Waters

- Electrolyte-Supporting Sips

Chapter 8: Batch Cooking and Meal Prep Made Simple

- Make-Ahead Zepbound Breakfasts

- Prep-Ahead Lunches in Jars

- Freezer-Friendly Dinners

Chapter 9: Dining Out While on Zepbound

- How to Read Menus and Choose Wisely

- Best Restaurant Swaps

- Tips for Social Events and Travel

Chapter 10: Special Diet Variations (Gluten-Free, Dairy-Free, Vegan-Friendly)

- Zepbound Recipes for Food Sensitivities

- Plant-Based Protein Options

BONUS CHAPTER

Bonus 2: Weekly and Monthly Shopping Lists

- Ingredient Swap Chart for Common Cravings

- Portion Control and Food Journal Templates

Chapter 1

Zepbound Basics in the Kitchen

The Zepbound-Friendly Pantry

Zucchini Noodle Stir-Fry

Ingredients:

- 2 medium zucchinis, spiralized
- 1 tbsp avocado oil
- ½ cup sliced bell peppers
- ¼ cup chopped scallions
- 1 tsp grated ginger
- 1 clove garlic, minced
- 1 tbsp coconut aminos
- 1 tsp sesame seeds

Instructions:

Heat avocado oil in a skillet over medium heat. Add garlic, ginger, and scallions; sauté for 1–2 minutes. Add bell peppers and cook for 3 minutes. Toss in zucchini noodles and coconut aminos, stir-frying until tender but not soggy. Sprinkle with sesame seeds before serving.

Crispy Chickpea Snack Jars

Ingredients:

- 1 can chickpeas, drained and rinsed
- 1 tbsp olive oil
- 1 tsp smoked paprika
- ½ tsp sea salt
- ½ tsp garlic powder

Instructions:

Preheat oven to 400°F (200°C). Pat chickpeas dry and spread on a baking sheet. Toss with oil and spices. Roast for 30–35 minutes, shaking the pan halfway through, until crispy. Store in glass jars for grab-and-go pantry snacks.

Chia-Flax Bread Bites

Ingredients:

- 1 cup almond flour

- 2 tbsp chia seeds

- 2 tbsp ground flaxseed

- 1 tsp baking powder

- ¼ tsp sea salt

- 3 eggs

- 2 tbsp olive oil

- ¼ cup unsweetened almond milk

Instructions:

Preheat oven to 350°F (175°C). Mix all ingredients in a bowl. Let sit for 10 minutes to thicken. Pour into a greased mini muffin tin. Bake for 20 minutes or until tops are golden and a toothpick comes out clean. Cool and store airtight.

Cooking Oils, Herbs, and Spices That Support Metabolic Health

Herbed Olive Oil Dip

Ingredients:

- ¼ cup extra virgin olive oil

- 1 tsp dried oregano

- ½ tsp rosemary

- ½ tsp thyme

- Pinch red pepper flakes

- ¼ tsp sea salt

- 1 garlic clove, grated

Instructions:

Mix all ingredients in a small bowl. Let rest for 10 minutes to infuse. Serve as a dip for raw veggies or drizzle over roasted dishes.

Golden Turmeric Tahini Dressing

Ingredients:

- 3 tbsp tahini

- 1 tbsp olive oil

- 1 tsp turmeric

- ½ tsp cumin

- Juice of 1 lemon

- 1 tbsp water

- Salt to taste

Instructions:

Whisk all ingredients together in a small bowl. Add more water to thin if needed. Store in a glass jar and use over roasted vegetables or salads.

Spiced Coconut Veggie Bake

Ingredients:

- 1 cup chopped cauliflower

- 1 cup chopped broccoli

- ½ cup diced carrots

- 1 tbsp coconut oil

- ½ tsp curry powder

- ¼ tsp cinnamon

- Salt and pepper to taste

Instructions:

Preheat oven to 375°F (190°C). Melt coconut oil and toss with veggies and spices. Spread on a lined baking sheet. Roast for 25–30 minutes until golden and crisp on edges. Serve hot or cold.

Avocado Cilantro Sauce

Ingredients:

- 1 ripe avocado

- ¼ cup fresh cilantro

- Juice of 1 lime

- 1 garlic clove

- 2 tbsp olive oil

- 2 tbsp water

- Sea salt to taste

Instructions:

Blend all ingredients in a food processor until creamy. Use as a topping for grilled proteins, wraps, or veggie bowls.

Portion Guidance and Macronutrient Balancing

High-Protein Breakfast Bowl

Ingredients:

- 2 boiled eggs

- ½ avocado, sliced

- ½ cup sautéed spinach

- ¼ cup cooked quinoa

- 1 tbsp pumpkin seeds

- Dash sea salt

- 1 tsp olive oil

Instructions:

Layer all ingredients in a bowl. Drizzle with olive oil and sprinkle with salt. Perfect for portion-controlled, balanced macros to start your day.

Balanced Plate Chicken and Veggies

Ingredients:

- 4 oz grilled chicken breast

- ½ cup steamed broccoli

- ½ cup roasted sweet potato

- 1 tbsp olive oil

- Salt and pepper to taste

Instructions:

Arrange components in a divided plate to guide portions. Drizzle with olive oil before serving. Ideal for lunch or dinner with clean macronutrient ratios.

Mini Protein Frittatas

Ingredients:

- 6 eggs

- ½ cup chopped spinach

- ¼ cup diced red pepper

- ¼ cup shredded zucchini

- Salt and black pepper

- 1 tbsp avocado oil

Instructions:

Preheat oven to 350°F (175°C). Whisk eggs and mix in vegetables. Grease a muffin tin with avocado oil. Pour mixture into each cup and bake 20–22 minutes. Store in the fridge for a quick protein portion anytime.

Protein-Packed Zucchini Boats

Ingredients:

- 2 medium zucchinis, halved lengthwise

- 1 cup cooked ground turkey

- ¼ cup diced tomatoes

- 1 tsp Italian seasoning

- 1 tbsp olive oil

- Salt and pepper to taste

Instructions:

Preheat oven to 375°F (190°C). Scoop out the center of zucchinis to form boats. Mix turkey, tomatoes, seasoning, and oil. Fill zucchini and bake for 25 minutes. Serve with a side of leafy greens.

Almond Butter Protein Balls

Ingredients:

- ½ cup almond butter

- ¼ cup ground flaxseed

- 2 tbsp chia seeds

- 2 tbsp collagen peptides (optional)

- 1 tbsp cocoa powder

- 1 tbsp monk fruit sweetener

- Pinch of sea salt

Instructions:

Mix all ingredients in a bowl. Roll into small balls and refrigerate. One or two balls equals a perfect fat-protein snack portion.

Balanced Berry Yogurt Parfait

Ingredients:

- ½ cup unsweetened coconut yogurt

- ¼ cup fresh berries

- 1 tbsp hemp seeds

- 1 tbsp chia seeds

- 1 tsp cinnamon

Instructions:

Layer yogurt, berries, and seeds in a small jar. Sprinkle with cinnamon. Great as a high-fiber snack or mini meal.

Quinoa-Lentil Salad Jar

Ingredients:

- ½ cup cooked quinoa

- ½ cup cooked green lentils

- ¼ cup diced cucumber

- ¼ cup cherry tomatoes

- 1 tbsp olive oil

- Juice of ½ lemon

- Salt and pepper

Instructions:

Layer all ingredients in a mason jar. Shake before eating. Keeps well in the fridge for 3–4 days. Ideal for meal prep and portion control.

Salmon Sheet Pan Dinner

Ingredients:

- 1 salmon fillet (4–6 oz)

- ½ cup broccoli florets

- ½ cup sliced zucchini

- 1 tbsp olive oil

- 1 tsp garlic powder

- 1 tsp lemon zest

- Salt and pepper

Instructions:

Preheat oven to 400°F (200°C). Line a sheet pan and place salmon and vegetables. Drizzle with olive oil and season with garlic, lemon zest, salt, and pepper. Roast for 15–20 minutes. A one-pan solution for macronutrient balance.

Egg Roll in a Bowl

Ingredients:

- 1 cup shredded cabbage

- ½ cup ground chicken

- 1 clove garlic, minced

- 1 tsp ginger

- 1 tbsp coconut aminos

- 1 tsp sesame oil

- Green onions for garnish

Instructions:

Cook ground chicken in a skillet. Add garlic, ginger, and cabbage. Stir-fry for 5–6 minutes. Add coconut aminos and sesame oil. Top with green onions before serving.

Cauliflower Rice Power Bowl

Ingredients:

- 1 cup cauliflower rice

- ½ cup black beans

- ¼ avocado

- 2 tbsp salsa

- 1 tbsp olive oil

- Lime wedge

- Salt and pepper

Instructions:

Warm the cauliflower rice and black beans. Top with avocado, salsa, oil, and a squeeze of lime. A fiber-packed, plant-based option with clean macros.

Chapter 2

Breakfasts to Boost Metabolism

Protein-Packed Morning Bowls

Smoked Salmon Avocado Bowl

Ingredients:

- 2 oz smoked wild salmon
- ½ avocado, sliced
- ½ cup sautéed kale
- 1 boiled egg, halved
- 1 tbsp hemp seeds
- 1 tsp olive oil
- Sea salt and black pepper

Instructions:

Layer kale at the base of a bowl. Top with salmon, avocado, and egg halves. Drizzle with olive oil, sprinkle hemp seeds, and season with salt and pepper.

Quinoa and Turkey Breakfast Bowl

Ingredients:

- ½ cup cooked quinoa

- 2 oz ground turkey, cooked with salt and pepper

- ½ cup sautéed spinach

- 1 tbsp pumpkin seeds

- 1 tsp coconut aminos

- Pinch of smoked paprika

Instructions:

Assemble quinoa, turkey, and spinach in a bowl. Top with seeds and coconut aminos. Dust with paprika and serve warm.

Tofu Power Scramble Bowl

Ingredients:

- ½ block firm tofu, crumbled

- ¼ tsp turmeric

- ½ cup diced zucchini

- ½ cup chopped red bell pepper

- 1 tsp olive oil

- Salt and pepper

- 1 tbsp nutritional yeast

Instructions:

Heat oil and sauté veggies for 3–4 minutes. Add tofu, turmeric, salt, and pepper. Cook until slightly crispy. Sprinkle nutritional yeast on top before serving.

Cottage Cheese Berry Bowl

Ingredients:

- ½ cup full-fat cottage cheese

- ¼ cup blueberries

- ¼ cup raspberries

- 1 tbsp ground flaxseed

- 1 tbsp chopped walnuts

- Dash of cinnamon

Instructions:

Combine all ingredients in a bowl. Stir gently and enjoy chilled.

Chia-Protein Breakfast Pudding

Ingredients:

- 3 tbsp chia seeds

- ¾ cup unsweetened almond milk

- ½ scoop vanilla protein powder

- 1 tbsp almond butter

- 1 tsp cinnamon

- 1 tbsp cacao nibs

Instructions:

Mix almond milk and protein powder until smooth. Stir in chia seeds, almond butter, and cinnamon. Refrigerate overnight. Top with cacao nibs before serving.

Egg-Based Dishes with Veggie Power

Spinach and Mushroom Egg Muffins

Ingredients:

- 6 eggs

- ½ cup chopped spinach

- ½ cup diced mushrooms

- ¼ cup chopped red onions

- Salt and pepper

- 1 tbsp avocado oil

Instructions:

Preheat oven to 350°F (175°C). Whisk eggs and mix in veggies. Grease muffin tin with oil and fill cups ¾ full. Bake for 20 minutes or until centers are firm.

Avocado Egg Skillet

Ingredients:

- 2 eggs

- ½ avocado, sliced

- 1 cup arugula

- 1 tbsp olive oil

- 1 tsp lemon juice

- Salt and crushed red pepper

Instructions:

Heat oil in a skillet. Add arugula and cook for 1 minute. Crack eggs on top and cook to desired doneness. Add avocado and lemon juice before serving.

Zucchini Noodle Egg Nest

Ingredients:

- 1 medium zucchini, spiralized

- 2 eggs

- 1 tbsp olive oil

- 1 garlic clove, minced

- Salt and pepper

- 1 tbsp parmesan (optional)

Instructions:

Sauté garlic in olive oil. Add zucchini noodles and cook for 2 minutes. Shape into a nest and crack eggs in the center. Cover and cook until eggs are set. Sprinkle with parmesan if using.

Southwest Veggie Omelet

Ingredients:

- 3 eggs

- ¼ cup chopped tomatoes

- ¼ cup diced bell peppers

- 1 tbsp chopped jalapeño

- 2 tbsp shredded non-dairy cheese

- 1 tsp avocado oil

- Salt and pepper

Instructions:

Heat oil in a skillet. Sauté veggies for 2 minutes. Pour in whisked eggs and cook until set. Add cheese and fold over. Cook for another minute and serve hot.

Broccoli Cheddar Scramble

Ingredients:

- 3 eggs

- ½ cup steamed chopped broccoli

- 2 tbsp shredded cheddar (or dairy-free alternative)

- 1 tbsp olive oil

- Salt and pepper

Instructions:

Whisk eggs and set aside. Heat oil in a pan, add broccoli, then pour in eggs. Stir continuously until eggs are soft-scrambled. Add cheese and cook until melted.

Mediterranean Egg White Wrap

Ingredients:

- ½ cup egg whites

- ¼ cup diced cucumber

- 2 tbsp chopped olives

- 2 tbsp crumbled feta

- ½ tsp oregano

- 1 coconut or almond flour wrap

Instructions:

Cook egg whites in a skillet until set. Fill wrap with eggs and other ingredients. Roll and serve warm or cold.

Bell Pepper Egg Rings

Ingredients:

- 1 bell pepper, sliced into ½-inch rings

- 2 eggs

- 1 tsp olive oil

- Salt and pepper

- Chopped parsley

Instructions:

Heat oil in a skillet. Place pepper rings and crack an egg into each. Cover and cook until set. Sprinkle with parsley and serve.

Low-Carb Pancakes and Grain-Free Oatmeal Alternatives

Almond Flour Pancakes

Ingredients:

- ½ cup almond flour

- 2 eggs

- 1 tbsp coconut flour

- 1 tsp baking powder

- 1 tsp vanilla

- ¼ cup unsweetened almond milk

Instructions:

Mix all ingredients. Heat nonstick skillet over medium heat. Spoon batter to form pancakes. Cook 2–3 minutes per side. Serve with nut butter or fresh berries.

Flaxseed Protein Pancakes

Ingredients:

- 2 tbsp ground flaxseed

- 1 egg

- ½ scoop vanilla protein powder

- 2 tbsp almond flour

- ¼ cup almond milk

- Cinnamon to taste

Instructions:

Combine ingredients into a batter. Let sit for 5 minutes to thicken. Cook on a lightly oiled skillet for 2 minutes per side. Stack and serve warm.

Cauliflower Oat-Free Porridge

Ingredients:

- ½ cup riced cauliflower

- ½ cup coconut milk

- 1 tbsp almond butter

- 1 tbsp chia seeds

- ½ tsp cinnamon

- Stevia or monk fruit to taste

Instructions:

Simmer cauliflower and coconut milk for 5–6 minutes. Stir in chia, almond butter, cinnamon, and sweetener. Cook until thickened. Serve warm with a sprinkle of hemp seeds.

Zucchini Cinnamon "Oats"

Ingredients:

- ½ cup shredded zucchini

- 1 egg

- ¼ cup unsweetened almond milk

- 1 tbsp flaxseed meal

- 1 tsp cinnamon

- Vanilla extract

- Monk fruit sweetener

Instructions:

In a small pot, combine all ingredients. Stir continuously over medium heat until mixture thickens like oatmeal (5–7 minutes). Top with a dollop of nut butter or berries.

Coconut Chia Breakfast Bowl

Ingredients:

- 3 tbsp chia seeds

- 1 cup coconut milk

- 1 tbsp shredded coconut

- 1 tsp vanilla extract

- 1 tbsp chopped almonds

- Dash cinnamon

Instructions:

Mix all ingredients in a jar. Refrigerate overnight. Stir and top with extra coconut or nuts before eating.

Pecan Pumpkin Pancakes

Ingredients:

- ½ cup canned pumpkin

- 2 eggs

- 2 tbsp coconut flour

- 1 tbsp chopped pecans

- ½ tsp pumpkin pie spice

- ¼ tsp baking powder

- 1 tsp vanilla extract

Instructions:

Mix ingredients into a batter. Heat skillet over medium and spoon batter to make small pancakes. Cook 3 minutes per side. Serve with a drizzle of almond butter.

Nut-Free Banana "N'oatmeal"

Ingredients:

- 1 ripe banana, mashed

- 1 tbsp sunflower seed butter

- 2 tbsp hemp seeds

- 1 tbsp chia seeds

- ¼ cup unsweetened hemp milk

- Dash cinnamon

Instructions:

Stir all ingredients together in a saucepan. Heat over medium until thick and warm. Serve in a bowl with sliced strawberries.

Keto Matcha Mug Pancake

Ingredients:

- 1 egg

- 2 tbsp almond flour

- 1 tsp matcha powder

- 1 tbsp coconut oil

- ½ tsp baking powder

- Stevia to taste

Instructions:

Mix all ingredients in a mug. Microwave for 1–2 minutes until set. Turn out onto a plate and top with coconut yogurt or berries.

Chapter 3

Smart Lunches for Lasting Energy

Satisfying Salads with Healthy Fats

Avocado and Salmon Power Salad

Ingredients:

- 2 cups mixed greens
- 4 oz grilled wild-caught salmon
- ½ avocado, sliced
- 1 tbsp hemp seeds
- 1 tbsp pumpkin seeds
- 1 tbsp olive oil
- Juice of ½ lemon
- Pinch sea salt

Instructions:

Place greens in a bowl. Top with grilled salmon, avocado, hemp seeds, and pumpkin seeds. Drizzle with olive oil and lemon juice. Sprinkle with salt and serve immediately.

Greek-Inspired Olive and Feta Salad

Ingredients:

- 2 cups chopped romaine

- ¼ cup crumbled sheep's milk feta

- ¼ cup sliced kalamata olives

- ¼ cup cherry tomatoes, halved

- 2 tbsp diced cucumber

- 1 tbsp olive oil

- 1 tbsp red wine vinegar

- ½ tsp dried oregano

Instructions:

Combine romaine, feta, olives, tomatoes, and cucumber in a bowl. Whisk oil, vinegar, and oregano. Drizzle over salad and toss gently.

Egg and Avocado Spinach Salad

Ingredients:

- 2 cups baby spinach

- 2 hard-boiled eggs, sliced

- ½ avocado, diced

- 1 tbsp sunflower seeds

- 1 tbsp olive oil

- 1 tsp Dijon mustard

- Pinch black pepper

Instructions:

Arrange spinach in a bowl. Top with eggs, avocado, and sunflower seeds. Mix oil, mustard, and pepper for the dressing. Drizzle and serve.

Walnut and Pear Arugula Salad

Ingredients:

- 2 cups arugula

- ½ ripe pear, sliced

- 2 tbsp chopped walnuts

- 1 tbsp goat cheese (optional)

- 1 tbsp olive oil

- 1 tsp balsamic vinegar

Instructions:

Toss arugula, pear, walnuts, and goat cheese in a bowl. Mix oil and vinegar and drizzle over the salad.

Southwest Avocado Chicken Salad

Ingredients:

- 2 cups chopped romaine

- ½ cup cooked chicken breast, diced

- ¼ avocado, cubed

- 2 tbsp black beans

- 1 tbsp lime juice

- 1 tbsp olive oil

- 1 tbsp chopped cilantro

Instructions:

Combine all ingredients in a large bowl. Toss to combine. Serve immediately or chill before serving.

Wraps and Bowls with Lean Protein and Fiber

Grilled Chicken Collard Wraps

Ingredients:

- 2 large collard green leaves

- 4 oz grilled chicken breast, sliced

- ¼ avocado, mashed

- ¼ cup shredded carrots

- 2 tbsp hummus

- Dash paprika

Instructions:

Spread hummus and avocado on each collard leaf. Add chicken and carrots. Sprinkle with paprika. Roll up tightly and slice in half.

Lentil and Quinoa Protein Bowl

Ingredients:

- ½ cup cooked quinoa

- ½ cup cooked green lentils

- ½ cup steamed broccoli

- 1 tbsp tahini

- Juice of ½ lemon

- Pinch cumin and sea salt

Instructions:

Layer quinoa, lentils, and broccoli in a bowl. Mix tahini, lemon, cumin, and salt for dressing. Drizzle and serve warm or cold.

Turkey and Veggie Lettuce Cups

Ingredients:

- 4 large romaine or butter lettuce leaves

- ½ cup ground turkey, cooked

- 2 tbsp diced bell pepper

- 1 tbsp chopped red onion

- 1 tbsp salsa

- 1 tsp olive oil

Instructions:

Fill each lettuce leaf with ground turkey, peppers, and onion. Drizzle with salsa and olive oil. Fold and eat like tacos.

Tuna and White Bean Bowl

Ingredients:

- 1 can tuna in olive oil, drained

- ½ cup canned white beans, rinsed

- ¼ cup chopped celery

- 1 tbsp lemon juice

- 1 tbsp olive oil

- Pinch dried dill

Instructions:

Mix all ingredients in a bowl. Serve over a bed of greens or with cucumber slices on the side.

Tempeh Avocado Bowl

Ingredients:

- ½ cup cooked tempeh, cubed

- ¼ avocado, diced

- ½ cup cooked brown rice or cauliflower rice

- ¼ cup steamed kale

- 1 tbsp coconut aminos

Instructions:

Arrange tempeh, avocado, rice, and kale in a bowl. Drizzle with coconut aminos and mix gently.

Boiled Egg Veggie Wrap

Ingredients:

- 2 hard-boiled eggs, chopped

- 1 tbsp Greek yogurt (or dairy-free yogurt)

- ¼ cup shredded carrots

- 2 tbsp diced cucumber

- 1 tbsp chopped parsley

- Salt and pepper

- 2 coconut or almond wraps

Instructions:

Mash eggs with yogurt, mix in vegetables and herbs. Season to taste. Fill wraps and roll tightly.

Chickpea Salad Wraps

Ingredients:

- ½ cup canned chickpeas, mashed

- 1 tbsp tahini

- 1 tbsp lemon juice

- 1 tbsp chopped celery

- 1 tbsp chopped red onion

- 2 large romaine leaves or collard greens

Instructions:

Mix chickpeas with tahini, lemon, and veggies. Scoop into the greens and wrap like a burrito.

Low-Glycemic Soups and Stews

Coconut-Curry Lentil Soup

Ingredients:

- ½ cup red lentils

- 1 cup chopped zucchini

- ½ cup diced tomatoes

- 2 cups vegetable broth

- ¼ cup coconut milk

- 1 tsp curry powder

- ½ tsp turmeric

- 1 tbsp olive oil

Instructions:

Sauté zucchini in oil for 5 minutes. Add lentils, tomatoes, spices, and broth. Simmer 20–25 minutes. Stir in coconut milk and cook 5 more minutes.

Creamy Cauliflower Soup

Ingredients:

- 2 cups cauliflower florets

- ½ small onion, chopped

- 2 cups low-sodium broth

- ¼ cup coconut milk

- 1 garlic clove

- 1 tbsp olive oil

- Salt and pepper

Instructions:

Sauté onion and garlic in oil. Add cauliflower and broth. Simmer until soft. Blend until smooth. Stir in coconut milk and season.

Chicken and Kale Stew

Ingredients:

- 1 cup cooked shredded chicken
- 1 cup chopped kale
- 1 celery stalk, chopped
- ½ cup diced zucchini
- 3 cups chicken broth
- 1 tsp thyme
- Salt and pepper

Instructions:

Bring broth to a boil. Add vegetables and thyme. Simmer for 10 minutes. Add chicken and cook another 5 minutes.

Zucchini Noodle and Turkey Soup

Ingredients:

- 2 zucchinis, spiralized
- ½ cup ground turkey
- 1 garlic clove, minced

- 1 tbsp olive oil

- 3 cups bone broth

- Salt, pepper, basil to taste

Instructions:

Brown turkey in oil with garlic. Add broth and bring to boil. Add zucchini noodles and simmer for 5 minutes. Season with herbs.

Vegetable Detox Soup

Ingredients:

- ½ cup chopped carrots

- ½ cup chopped cabbage

- ¼ cup diced onions

- 1 celery stalk

- 2 cups vegetable broth

- 1 tsp grated ginger

- 1 tbsp olive oil

- Juice of ½ lemon

Instructions:

Sauté onion, ginger, and celery. Add remaining vegetables and broth. Simmer for 20 minutes. Add lemon juice before serving.

Miso-Ginger Mushroom Soup

Ingredients:

- 2 cups low-sodium vegetable broth
- ½ cup sliced mushrooms
- ½ cup chopped bok choy
- 1 tbsp miso paste
- 1 tsp grated ginger
- 1 tbsp sesame oil

Instructions:

Heat oil in a pot. Sauté ginger and mushrooms for 5 minutes. Add broth and bok choy. Dissolve miso paste in warm broth and stir into soup. Simmer for 5 more minutes.

Spiced Carrot and Lentil Soup

Ingredients:

- 1 cup chopped carrots

- ½ cup red lentils

- 1 small onion, chopped

- 1 garlic clove, minced

- 2 cups broth

- ½ tsp cumin

- 1 tbsp olive oil

- Salt and pepper

Instructions:

Sauté onion, garlic, and carrots in oil. Add lentils, broth, and cumin. Simmer for 20–25 minutes until soft. Blend half the soup for a creamier texture.

Chapter 4

Dinners That Burn Fat and Satisfy

Sheet Pan Meals and One-Pot Wonders

Sheet Pan Lemon-Dill Salmon with Asparagus

Ingredients:

- 2 salmon fillets (4 oz each)

- 1 bunch asparagus, trimmed

- 1 tbsp olive oil

- 1 tsp lemon zest

- Juice of 1 lemon

- 1 tsp dried dill

- Sea salt and black pepper

Instructions:

Preheat oven to 400°F (200°C). Arrange salmon and asparagus on a parchment-lined sheet pan. Drizzle with olive oil, lemon juice, and zest. Sprinkle with dill, salt, and pepper. Bake for 15–18 minutes or until salmon flakes easily.

One-Pot Ground Turkey and Zucchini Skillet

Ingredients:

- 1 lb ground turkey

- 2 medium zucchinis, chopped

- 1 cup diced tomatoes

- 1 tsp garlic powder

- 1 tsp onion powder

- ½ tsp smoked paprika

- Sea salt and pepper

- 1 tbsp olive oil

Instructions:

In a large skillet, heat olive oil over medium heat. Brown turkey until fully cooked. Add zucchini, tomatoes, and spices. Simmer for 10 minutes, stirring occasionally. Serve warm.

Sheet Pan Garlic-Lime Chicken and Cauliflower

Ingredients:

- 2 boneless, skinless chicken breasts

- 2 cups cauliflower florets

- Juice of 1 lime

- 2 garlic cloves, minced

- 1 tbsp avocado oil

- 1 tsp cumin

- Sea salt and pepper

Instructions:

Preheat oven to 375°F (190°C). Toss cauliflower and chicken in lime juice, garlic, oil, and cumin. Place on a baking sheet and roast for 25 minutes. Serve hot with a wedge of lime.

One-Pot Shrimp and Spinach Coconut Curry

Ingredients:

- 1 lb shrimp, peeled and deveined

- 2 cups spinach

- 1 can full-fat coconut milk

- 1 tbsp red curry paste

- 1 tsp ginger, grated

- 1 tbsp coconut oil

- Salt to taste

Instructions:

Heat coconut oil in a large skillet. Sauté curry paste and ginger for 1 minute. Add shrimp and cook until pink. Pour in coconut milk and stir in spinach. Simmer until spinach wilts and flavors meld, about 5 minutes.

Sheet Pan Chicken Fajitas

Ingredients:

- 2 chicken breasts, sliced

- 1 red bell pepper, sliced

- 1 green bell pepper, sliced

- 1 red onion, sliced

- 1 tbsp olive oil

- 1 tsp chili powder

- 1 tsp cumin

- ½ tsp garlic powder

- Salt and pepper

Instructions:

Preheat oven to 425°F (220°C). Toss all ingredients on a sheet pan. Spread evenly. Bake for 20 minutes, tossing halfway through. Serve in lettuce wraps or with cauliflower rice.

One-Pot Cauliflower Rice Stir-Fry with Chicken

Ingredients:

- 1 cup cauliflower rice

- 1 cup cooked chicken breast, shredded

- ½ cup chopped carrots

- ½ cup peas

- 2 eggs, scrambled

- 1 tbsp coconut aminos

- 1 tsp sesame oil

Instructions:

Sauté carrots and peas in sesame oil. Add cauliflower rice and heat for 3 minutes. Stir in chicken and coconut aminos. Push mixture aside and scramble eggs in the same pan. Mix everything together and serve hot.

Lean Protein + Veggie Combos

Turkey Cabbage Stir-Fry

Ingredients:

- 1 lb ground turkey

- 3 cups shredded green cabbage

- 1 tbsp coconut oil

- 1 tsp garlic powder

- 1 tsp ginger

- 1 tbsp coconut aminos

- Green onion for garnish

Instructions:

In a large pan, cook turkey until browned. Add cabbage, oil, and spices. Cook until cabbage softens, about 10 minutes. Stir in coconut aminos. Top with green onions.

Lemon-Garlic Cod with Broccoli Mash

Ingredients:

- 2 cod fillets

- Juice of 1 lemon

- 2 garlic cloves, minced

- 2 cups steamed broccoli

- 2 tbsp olive oil

- Salt and pepper

Instructions:

Mash steamed broccoli with 1 tbsp olive oil and salt. In a skillet, sear cod in remaining oil with lemon and garlic. Cook until fish is flaky. Serve over broccoli mash.

Chicken and Zoodle Power Bowl

Ingredients:

- 1 grilled chicken breast, sliced

- 2 medium zucchinis, spiralized

- ¼ avocado

- 1 tbsp olive oil

- 1 tsp dried oregano

- Sea salt and pepper

Instructions:

Sauté zoodles in olive oil for 2–3 minutes. Season with oregano, salt, and pepper. Top with chicken slices and avocado. Serve warm or chilled.

Spaghetti Squash Turkey Bolognese

Ingredients:

- 1 small spaghetti squash, roasted

- 1 lb ground turkey

- 1 cup tomato sauce (no sugar added)

- 1 tsp Italian seasoning

- 1 tbsp olive oil

- Salt and pepper

Instructions:

Roast squash at 400°F (200°C) for 35–40 minutes. Scrape into strands. Brown turkey in oil and stir in sauce and seasoning. Serve over squash noodles.

Grilled Tofu and Veggie Skewers

Ingredients:

- 1 block extra-firm tofu, cubed

- 1 zucchini, sliced

- 1 bell pepper, chopped

- 1 red onion, chopped

- 1 tbsp olive oil

- 1 tsp garlic powder

- 1 tsp paprika

Instructions:

Toss all ingredients. Thread onto skewers. Grill or bake at 375°F (190°C) for 20–25 minutes. Flip halfway through. Serve with a squeeze of lemon.

Flavorful, Low-Calorie Global-Inspired Plates

Moroccan Spiced Chicken with Cauliflower Couscous

Ingredients:

- 2 chicken thighs, skinless
- 1 tsp cumin
- 1 tsp cinnamon
- ½ tsp paprika
- 1 tbsp olive oil
- 1 cup cauliflower couscous
- 1 tbsp chopped parsley

Instructions:

Rub chicken with oil and spices. Roast at 400°F (200°C) for 25 minutes. Pulse cauliflower in food processor to couscous texture. Sauté in a dry skillet for 5 minutes. Garnish with parsley and plate with chicken.

Thai-Inspired Basil Beef Lettuce Wraps

Ingredients:

- ½ lb lean ground beef

- 1 tbsp coconut aminos

- 1 tsp fish sauce

- ½ tsp chili flakes

- ¼ cup chopped basil

- Butter lettuce leaves

Instructions:

Brown beef in a skillet. Add coconut aminos, fish sauce, and chili flakes. Stir in basil. Spoon into lettuce cups and serve immediately.

Greek Lemon Chicken Bowl

Ingredients:

- 1 grilled chicken breast

- ¼ cup chopped cucumber

- ¼ cup cherry tomatoes

- 2 tbsp red onion

- 1 tbsp olive oil

- Juice of ½ lemon

- ¼ tsp oregano

- Sea salt

Instructions:

Combine vegetables in a bowl. Add sliced chicken. Whisk lemon, oil, oregano, and salt into a dressing. Drizzle over the bowl before serving.

Korean-Inspired Cauliflower Bulgogi Bowl

Ingredients:

- 2 cups cauliflower rice

- 1 cup sliced mushrooms

- 1 cup shredded cabbage

- 2 tbsp coconut aminos

- 1 tsp sesame oil

- 1 tsp garlic

- ½ tsp ginger

Instructions:

Stir-fry mushrooms and cabbage in sesame oil. Add garlic, ginger, and coconut aminos. Serve hot over cauliflower rice.

Mexican Turkey Taco Bowl

Ingredients:

- 1 cup ground turkey

- ½ tsp cumin

- ½ tsp paprika

- ¼ tsp chili powder

- 1 cup shredded lettuce

- ¼ cup diced tomato

- 2 tbsp guacamole

Instructions:

Brown turkey with spices. Layer lettuce, tomato, and turkey in a bowl. Top with guacamole and serve.

Indian-Spiced Lentil and Spinach Stew

Ingredients:

- ½ cup red lentils

- 2 cups water

- 1 cup spinach

- 1 tsp turmeric

- 1 tsp cumin seeds

- 1 tbsp coconut oil

- Salt to taste

Instructions:

Simmer lentils in water with turmeric until soft. In another pan, heat oil and toast cumin. Add spinach and stir until wilted. Combine with lentils and simmer for 5 minutes. Serve hot.

Japanese-Inspired Ginger Miso Cod

Ingredients:

- 2 cod fillets

- 1 tbsp white miso paste

- 1 tsp grated ginger

- 1 tbsp coconut aminos

- 1 tsp rice vinegar

Instructions:

Mix miso, ginger, coconut aminos, and vinegar into a glaze. Brush over cod. Bake at 375°F (190°C) for 15–18 minutes. Serve with steamed bok choy.

Chapter 5

Snacks to Curb Cravings

No-Bake Energy Bites and Protein Balls

Coconut-Cacao Collagen Bites

Ingredients:

- 1 cup unsweetened shredded coconut

- ½ cup almond butter

- 2 tbsp cacao powder

- 2 tbsp collagen peptides

- 1 tbsp chia seeds

- 1 tsp vanilla extract

- 2 tbsp monk fruit syrup or stevia-sweetened syrup

- Pinch of sea salt

Instructions:

Mix all ingredients in a bowl until well combined. Roll into 1-inch balls. Chill in the refrigerator for 30 minutes to firm. Store in an airtight container for up to 5 days.

Pumpkin-Spice Protein Balls

Ingredients:

- ½ cup pumpkin purée

- ½ cup almond flour

- 2 tbsp ground flaxseed

- 1 scoop vanilla plant-based protein powder

- 1 tsp cinnamon

- ¼ tsp nutmeg

- 2 tbsp sunflower seed butter

- Stevia or monk fruit to taste

Instructions:

Combine all ingredients in a mixing bowl. Stir until a dough forms. Roll into balls and refrigerate. These are ideal pre-workout or afternoon pick-me-ups.

Lemon-Cashew Bliss Balls

Ingredients:

- 1 cup raw cashews

- Zest and juice of 1 lemon

- ½ cup coconut flour

- 1 tbsp coconut oil

- 1 tbsp honey or low-glycemic sweetener

- Pinch of sea salt

Instructions:

Pulse cashews in a food processor until fine. Add remaining ingredients and blend until dough forms. Roll into balls and chill.

Mocha Energy Bites

Ingredients:

- ½ cup rolled oats (gluten-free)

- ¼ cup almond butter

- 1 tbsp espresso or instant coffee powder

- 1 scoop chocolate protein powder

- 1 tbsp cocoa nibs

- 2 tbsp water

Instructions:

Combine all ingredients in a bowl. Mix thoroughly. Shape into bites and refrigerate to set. For best results, store in a sealed container for up to 4 days.

Tahini-Cinnamon Power Balls

Ingredients:

- ½ cup tahini

- 2 tbsp flaxseed meal

- 1 tbsp hemp seeds

- 1 tsp cinnamon

- 2 tbsp coconut flour

- 1 tbsp sugar-free maple syrup

Instructions:

Stir all ingredients together. Let the mixture sit for 5 minutes. Roll into balls and store in the fridge for a quick craving fix.

Crunchy Options with Fiber

Roasted Spiced Chickpeas

Ingredients:

- 1 can chickpeas, rinsed and dried

- 1 tbsp avocado oil

- 1 tsp paprika

- ½ tsp garlic powder

- ½ tsp cumin

- ¼ tsp cayenne

- ¼ tsp salt

Instructions:

Preheat oven to 400°F (200°C). Toss chickpeas with oil and spices. Spread on a baking sheet and roast for 30–35 minutes, shaking halfway. Cool completely for crunch. Store in a jar for snacking.

Crispy Kale Chips

Ingredients:

- 1 bunch kale, washed and torn

- 1 tbsp olive oil

- 1 tsp nutritional yeast

- ½ tsp garlic powder

- ¼ tsp salt

Instructions:

Preheat oven to 300°F (150°C). Massage kale with oil and seasonings. Spread on a parchment-lined sheet and bake for 20–25 minutes until crisp, rotating halfway. Cool before storing in a paper bag to maintain crispness.

Jicama and Cucumber Sticks with Guac Dip

Ingredients for Dip:

- 1 ripe avocado
- Juice of ½ lime
- 1 tbsp finely chopped red onion
- Salt and pepper to taste

For Dippers:

- 1 cup jicama, peeled and sliced
- 1 cup cucumber sticks

Instructions:

Mash avocado and mix with lime juice, onion, salt, and pepper. Serve with jicama and cucumber sticks for a hydrating, crunchy snack.

Chia Crackers

Ingredients:

- ½ cup chia seeds
- 1 cup water
- ½ tsp garlic powder

- ½ tsp onion powder

- ½ tsp sea salt

Instructions:

Soak chia seeds in water for 30 minutes until gelled. Spread thinly on a parchment-lined baking sheet. Sprinkle with seasoning. Bake at 325°F (160°C) for 35–40 minutes until crisp. Break into crackers and store airtight.

Toasted Coconut Chips

Ingredients:

- 1 cup unsweetened coconut flakes

- 1 tbsp coconut oil

- ½ tsp cinnamon

- 1 pinch sea salt

Instructions:

Preheat oven to 325°F (160°C). Toss flakes with oil and seasonings. Spread evenly on a baking sheet and toast for 5–7 minutes, stirring halfway. Cool completely before storing.

Zucchini Chips with Paprika

Ingredients:

- 1 medium zucchini, thinly sliced

- 1 tbsp olive oil

- 1 tsp smoked paprika

- Sea salt

Instructions:

Preheat oven to 225°F (110°C). Pat zucchini slices dry. Toss with oil, paprika, and salt. Bake on parchment-lined trays for 1½–2 hours, flipping halfway, until crisp. Cool before storing.

Nut-Free Trail Mix

Ingredients:

- ½ cup pumpkin seeds

- ½ cup sunflower seeds

- ¼ cup coconut flakes

- ¼ cup dried mulberries (unsweetened)

- 1 tbsp cacao nibs

Instructions:

Combine all ingredients and store in individual snack bags or jars. Ideal for fiber and mineral-rich, nut-free snacking.

Savory Low-Carb Bites for Midday Hunger

Mini Egg Muffins with Veggies

Ingredients:

- 4 eggs

- ¼ cup chopped spinach

- ¼ cup diced red bell pepper

- 2 tbsp diced onion

- Salt and pepper

- Olive oil spray

Instructions:

Preheat oven to 350°F (175°C). Whisk eggs with vegetables and seasonings. Spray a mini muffin tin and pour mixture in. Bake for 18–20 minutes until set. Store chilled and reheat as needed.

Turkey Cucumber Roll-Ups

Ingredients:

- 4 slices nitrate-free turkey breast

- ½ avocado, mashed

- ½ cucumber, sliced thin lengthwise

- 1 tbsp Dijon mustard

Instructions:

Spread mustard and avocado on turkey slices. Lay cucumber strips on top, roll tightly, and secure with toothpicks. High in protein, low in carbs.

Cauliflower Tots

Ingredients:

- 1 cup riced cauliflower

- 1 egg

- ¼ cup almond flour

- 2 tbsp nutritional yeast

- ½ tsp garlic powder

- ¼ tsp black pepper

Instructions:

Preheat oven to 375°F (190°C). Mix all ingredients in a bowl. Form into small tot shapes. Place on a parchment-lined tray and bake for 25 minutes, flipping halfway. Serve with low-sugar dipping sauce.

Stuffed Mini Bell Peppers

Ingredients:

- 6 mini bell peppers, halved and deseeded

- ½ cup hummus (or avocado mash)

- 1 tbsp chopped black olives

- 1 tsp za'atar or Italian seasoning

Instructions:

Fill pepper halves with hummus or avocado mash. Sprinkle with olives and herbs. Store chilled for savory, colorful bites.

Almond-Crusted Zucchini Sticks

Ingredients:

- 1 zucchini, sliced into sticks

- ¼ cup almond flour

- 1 egg, beaten

- ½ tsp garlic powder

- ¼ tsp paprika

- Salt to taste

Instructions:

Preheat oven to 400°F (200°C). Dip zucchini sticks in egg, then coat in seasoned almond flour. Bake for 20–25 minutes until golden and crisp. Serve warm or cold.

Hard-Boiled Egg & Guac Snack Box

Ingredients:

- 2 hard-boiled eggs

- ¼ cup guacamole

- 1 small handful baby carrots

Instructions:

Slice eggs in half and pack with guacamole and carrots in a bento-style box. Balanced with protein, healthy fats, and fiber.

Savory Seaweed Snack Wraps

Ingredients:

- 4 sheets roasted seaweed

- ½ avocado, mashed

- ½ cup shredded rotisserie chicken

- 1 tsp sesame seeds

Instructions:

Spread mashed avocado on seaweed. Add chicken, sprinkle sesame seeds, and roll tightly. Eat immediately or pack in a sealed container.

Zucchini Fritters

Ingredients:

- 1 cup shredded zucchini (squeezed dry)

- 1 egg

- 2 tbsp coconut flour

- 1 tbsp chopped scallions

- Salt and pepper

Instructions:

Mix all ingredients. Heat oil in a skillet over medium heat. Drop batter in small rounds and flatten. Cook for 2–3 minutes per side until golden. Cool and enjoy as a portable savory snack.

Spicy Tuna Lettuce Wraps

Ingredients:

- 1 small can tuna, drained

- 1 tbsp avocado oil mayo

- ½ tsp hot sauce (optional)

- Butter lettuce leaves

Instructions:

Mix tuna, mayo, and hot sauce. Scoop onto lettuce leaves and roll. Refreshing, satisfying, and ultra low-carb.

Chapter 6

Smoothies and Shakes for Fat Loss

Green Detox Smoothies

Spinach-Cucumber Cleansing Smoothie

Ingredients:

- 1 cup spinach

- ½ cucumber, peeled and sliced

- 1 stalk celery

- ½ green apple, chopped

- Juice of ½ lemon

- 1 tsp fresh grated ginger

- 1 cup cold water

- 4–5 ice cubes

Instructions:

Blend all ingredients until smooth. Serve immediately for a crisp, detoxifying start to your day.

Minty Avocado Detox Smoothie

Ingredients:

- ½ ripe avocado

- 1 cup romaine or spinach

- 1 tbsp lime juice

- 1 handful fresh mint

- ½ cup coconut water

- ½ cup water

- Ice to preference

Instructions:

Blend until creamy. This smoothie supports fat metabolism while soothing digestion.

Super Greens & Citrus Flush Smoothie

Ingredients:

- 1 cup kale

- ½ orange, peeled

- ½ grapefruit, peeled

- ½ frozen banana

- 1 tbsp ground flaxseed

- ½ cup unsweetened almond milk

- ½ cup cold water

Instructions:

Blend until smooth and frothy. The citrus pairs with greens for liver-loving benefits and a metabolism boost.

Celery-Lime Slim Smoothie

Ingredients:

- 1 cup chopped celery

- 1 small green apple

- ½ cucumber

- Juice of 1 lime

- 1 cup water

- 1 tbsp chia seeds

- Ice cubes

Instructions:

Blend and drink immediately. Ideal as a light, refreshing fat-burning mid-morning drink.

Zesty Green Pineapple Smoothie

Ingredients:

- 1 cup chopped pineapple

- 1 cup spinach

- ¼ avocado

- ½ tsp spirulina powder

- 1 tbsp hemp seeds

- 1 cup cold coconut water

Instructions:

Blend until smooth. Pineapple enzymes support digestion, while greens promote detoxification.

Cilantro-Cucumber Cleanse Smoothie

Ingredients:

- ½ cucumber

- ½ green pear

- Handful fresh cilantro

- Juice of ½ lemon

- 1 tbsp chia seeds

- 1 cup water

- 4–5 ice cubes

Instructions:

Blend thoroughly. Great for heavy-metal detox support and hydration.

Protein-Rich Meal Replacement Shakes

Vanilla-Coconut Fat-Burning Shake

Ingredients:

- 1 scoop plant-based vanilla protein powder

- 1 tbsp unsweetened shredded coconut

- 1 tbsp MCT oil

- ½ frozen banana

- 1 cup unsweetened almond milk

- 1 tbsp chia seeds

- ½ tsp cinnamon

Instructions:

Blend until creamy. Rich in healthy fats and protein to satisfy and fuel your fat-burning metabolism.

Chocolate Almond Butter Power Shake

Ingredients:

- 1 scoop chocolate protein powder

- 1 tbsp almond butter

- 1 tbsp ground flaxseed

- ½ cup frozen zucchini slices

- 1 cup unsweetened almond milk

- Dash of sea salt

- 1 tsp cacao nibs (optional topping)

Instructions:

Blend and serve thick. This shake mimics dessert without blood sugar spikes.

Berry-Omega Shake

Ingredients:

- ½ cup frozen mixed berries

- 1 scoop vanilla protein powder

- 1 tbsp ground flaxseed

- 1 tbsp hemp seeds

- 1 cup unsweetened oat milk

- 1 tsp lemon zest

Instructions:

Blend and sip chilled. Omega-3 fats and antioxidants work together to combat inflammation and boost metabolism.

Peanut Butter Cup Protein Shake (Zepbound-Friendly)

Ingredients:

- 1 scoop chocolate or peanut butter protein powder

- 1 tbsp powdered peanut butter or natural PB

- ½ frozen banana

- 1 tbsp chia seeds

- 1 cup unsweetened almond milk

- Ice cubes

Instructions:

Blend until smooth. Perfect for post-workout recovery or meal replacement with sustained energy.

Creamy Matcha Shake

Ingredients:

- 1 scoop unflavored or vanilla protein powder

- ½ tsp matcha powder

- ½ avocado

- 1 cup unsweetened almond or macadamia milk

- 1 tbsp MCT oil or coconut cream

- Stevia to taste

Instructions:

Blend until silky. Matcha promotes thermogenesis and energy without overstimulation.

Pumpkin Spice Protein Smoothie

Ingredients:

- ½ cup pumpkin purée

- 1 scoop vanilla protein powder

- 1 tsp pumpkin spice

- 1 tbsp ground flaxseed

- 1 cup unsweetened almond milk

- 1 tsp vanilla extract

- Stevia or monk fruit to taste

Instructions:

Blend until thick. A fall-flavored meal replacement that stabilizes glucose and satisfies.

Cinnamon Roll Shake

Ingredients:

- 1 scoop vanilla protein powder

- 1 tsp cinnamon

- 1 tsp ground flaxseed

- ½ frozen banana

- 1 cup unsweetened oat milk

- 1 tsp vanilla extract

Instructions:

Blend and garnish with a sprinkle of cinnamon. Ideal for breakfast on-the-go with balanced macros.

Smoothie Add-Ins That Support Zepbound's Effects

Fat-Burning Green Booster Smoothie

Ingredients:

- 1 scoop unflavored collagen or protein

- ½ avocado

- 1 tbsp MCT oil

- 1 cup spinach

- ½ cucumber

- Juice of ½ lemon

- Pinch of cayenne

- 1 cup cold water

Instructions:

Blend well. Cayenne, healthy fats, and greens support GLP-1 activation naturally.

Anti-Bloat Ginger-Berry Smoothie

Ingredients:

- ½ cup blueberries

- 1 scoop vanilla protein

- 1 tbsp chia seeds

- ½ tsp grated ginger

- 1 tbsp apple cider vinegar

- 1 cup unsweetened almond milk

Instructions:

Blend until frothy. This combo improves digestion and reduces water retention.

Appetite Control Cinnamon-Coffee Smoothie

Ingredients:

- 1 scoop chocolate protein powder

- ½ cup chilled brewed coffee

- ½ frozen banana

- ½ tsp cinnamon

- 1 tbsp ground flaxseed

- ½ cup unsweetened almond milk

- Stevia to taste

Instructions:

Blend smooth. Perfect morning shake for natural appetite regulation and fat loss.

Fiber-Rich Chia Greens Smoothie

Ingredients:

- 1 cup kale

- 1 tbsp chia seeds

- ½ green apple

- Juice of ½ lime

- 1 cup water

- ½ scoop collagen or fiber supplement

Instructions:

Blend well. This supports satiety and gut health—two key allies in Zepbound-enhanced weight loss.

Hormone-Friendly Cacao-Flax Smoothie

Ingredients:

- 1 scoop chocolate plant-based protein

- 1 tbsp ground flaxseed

- 1 tsp raw cacao

- ½ frozen banana

- 1 cup unsweetened macadamia milk

- Stevia or monk fruit to taste

Instructions:

Blend until thick and creamy. This nutrient-dense smoothie supports hormonal balance and reduces cravings.

Liver Support Beet-Berry Smoothie

Ingredients:

- ¼ cup cooked beetroot

- ½ cup blueberries

- ½ cup unsweetened almond milk

- ½ frozen banana

- 1 tbsp hemp seeds

- Juice of ½ lemon

Instructions:

Blend thoroughly. Beetroot supports detox, while berries and lemon add a fat-flushing antioxidant punch.

Zepbound Reset Citrus Smoothie

Ingredients:

- ½ grapefruit, peeled

- ½ lemon, juiced

- ½ cup cucumber

- 1 tbsp apple cider vinegar

- ½ inch fresh ginger

- 1 tbsp chia or flaxseed

- 1 cup water

Instructions:

Blend and serve over ice. The citrus-ginger-ACV combo amplifies Zepbound's appetite and metabolism benefits.

Chapter 7

Juices and Sips for Hydration and Blood Sugar Balance

Low-Sugar Vegetable Juices

Cucumber-Celery Juice with Lemon

Ingredients:

- 2 large cucumbers

- 3 celery stalks

- Juice of 1 lemon

- 1-inch piece fresh ginger

- ½ cup cold water

Instructions:

Juice cucumbers, celery, and ginger. Stir in lemon juice and water. Serve cold over ice. This ultra-hydrating juice is naturally low in sugar and high in potassium.

Green Pepper & Kale Metabolic Juice

Ingredients:

- 1 green bell pepper

- 1 cup kale

- 1 cucumber

- Juice of ½ lime

- ¼ tsp cayenne (optional)

- ½ cup water

Instructions:

Juice pepper, kale, and cucumber. Add lime juice, cayenne, and water. Shake or stir well before drinking. The bitterness balances blood sugar and reduces cravings.

Zucchini-Spinach Flush Juice

Ingredients:

- 1 small zucchini

- 1 handful spinach

- 1 green apple (optional for mild sweetness)

- Juice of ½ lemon

- ½ cup water

Instructions:

Juice zucchini, spinach, and apple. Stir in lemon juice and water. Sip slowly on an empty stomach for maximum cleansing benefits.

Tomato-Basil Detox Juice

Ingredients:

- 2 medium tomatoes

- ½ red bell pepper

- 1 stalk celery

- 1 tsp apple cider vinegar

- 3–4 fresh basil leaves

- ¼ tsp sea salt

- ½ cup cold water

Instructions:

Juice tomatoes, pepper, and celery. Blend in basil and ACV. Add salt and water. Serve chilled. This savory option supports hydration and satiety.

Asparagus-Celery Cleanse Juice

Ingredients:

- 6 asparagus spears

- 3 celery stalks

- Juice of ½ lemon

- 1-inch piece fresh turmeric

- ½ green apple (optional)

Instructions:

Juice all ingredients. Drink immediately to benefit from blood-sugar-stabilizing minerals and antioxidants.

Radish-Kale Metabolic Juice

Ingredients:

- 3 red radishes

- 1 cup kale

- ½ cucumber

- Juice of ½ lemon

- ½ tsp grated ginger

- ¼ cup cold water

Instructions:

Juice radishes, kale, and cucumber. Mix with lemon, ginger, and water. This juice promotes liver detox and blood sugar regulation naturally.

Fennel-Cucumber Cool Juice

Ingredients:

- 1 small fennel bulb

- 1 cucumber

- ½ lemon, juiced

- ½ cup cold water

Instructions:

Juice fennel and cucumber, then stir in lemon juice and water. This naturally sweet juice hydrates while soothing the digestive tract.

Herbal Teas and Infused Waters

Mint-Ginger Digestion Tea

Ingredients:

- 1 tbsp fresh mint leaves

- 1-inch fresh ginger, sliced

- 2 cups water

Instructions:

Simmer mint and ginger in water for 10 minutes. Strain and serve warm or chilled. Supports digestion and balances blood sugar after meals.

Cinnamon-Bay Leaf Glucose Tea

Ingredients:

- 1 cinnamon stick

- 2 bay leaves

- 2 cups water

Instructions:

Simmer cinnamon and bay leaves for 15 minutes. Remove and let cool slightly. Drink before or after meals to help lower glucose spikes.

Lemon Balm-Calm Tea

Ingredients:

- 1 tbsp dried lemon balm

- 2 cups boiling water

Instructions:

Steep lemon balm for 7–10 minutes. Strain and sip warm. Lemon balm supports stress balance, which indirectly improves glucose control.

Turmeric-Pepper Anti-Inflammatory Tea

Ingredients:

- 1 tsp ground turmeric

- Pinch of black pepper

- 1 cup hot water

- Juice of ½ lemon

Instructions:

Whisk turmeric and pepper into hot water. Add lemon juice. Sip slowly. Anti-inflammatory and blood sugar friendly.

Basil-Ginger Cooling Infusion

Ingredients:

- 5 basil leaves

- ½ inch fresh ginger

- 2 cups cold water

Instructions:

Crush basil and ginger, then steep in cold water for at least 2 hours in the fridge. Strain and serve chilled. Refreshing and supportive for blood sugar.

Apple Cider Vinegar Cinnamon Tonic

Ingredients:

- 1 tbsp apple cider vinegar

- ¼ tsp cinnamon

- Juice of ½ lemon

- 1 cup cold water

- Stevia (optional)

Instructions:

Mix all ingredients and stir well. Drink before meals to help stabilize postprandial glucose levels.

Cucumber-Mint Infused Water

Ingredients:

- ½ cucumber, sliced

- 5 mint leaves

- 3 cups cold water

Instructions:

Add cucumber and mint to water and refrigerate for 2+ hours. Drink throughout the day to encourage hydration and metabolic support.

Grapefruit-Rosemary Infused Water

Ingredients:

- ½ grapefruit, sliced

- 1 small sprig rosemary

- 3 cups cold water

Instructions:

Combine ingredients and chill for a few hours. Grapefruit contains compounds that support insulin sensitivity and rosemary reduces inflammation.

Lime-Ginger Sparkling Infusion

Ingredients:

- Juice of 1 lime

- 1-inch ginger, sliced

- 1 can plain sparkling water

Instructions:

Muddle lime and ginger together, then add sparkling water. Serve over ice for a hydrating, glucose-friendly beverage.

Electrolyte-Supporting Sips

Coconut-Lime Hydration Tonic

Ingredients:

- 1 cup coconut water

- Juice of ½ lime

- Pinch of sea salt

- Stevia or monk fruit to taste

Instructions:

Stir all ingredients together and drink post-exercise or first thing in the morning for rapid rehydration and mineral balance.

Chia-Citrus Electrolyte Drink

Ingredients:

- 1 tbsp chia seeds

- Juice of 1 lemon

- Juice of ½ orange

- 1½ cups cold water

- Pinch of Himalayan salt

Instructions:

Combine all ingredients and let sit for 10 minutes for chia to gel. Shake or stir before drinking. Supports sustained hydration and energy.

Watermelon-Cucumber Electrolyte Juice

Ingredients:

- 1 cup chopped watermelon

- ½ cucumber

- Pinch of sea salt

- Juice of ½ lime

Instructions:

Blend all ingredients, then strain if desired. Drink immediately for a refreshing, mineral-rich sip without added sugar.

Strawberry-Basil Electro-Infusion

Ingredients:

- ½ cup sliced strawberries

- 4–5 basil leaves

- ¼ tsp sea salt

- 3 cups water

Instructions:

Infuse ingredients in cold water for 2–3 hours. Basil enhances flavor while the salt restores lost electrolytes naturally.

Cucumber-Aloe Replenish Water

Ingredients:

- 1 tbsp aloe vera gel (pure, food grade)

- ½ cucumber

- Juice of ½ lemon

- 2 cups water

- Pinch of sea salt

Instructions:

Blend cucumber with water, strain, then stir in aloe, lemon, and salt. Chill and sip slowly for skin and blood sugar benefits.

Cranberry Electrolyte Flush

Ingredients:

- ¼ cup pure, unsweetened cranberry juice

- Juice of ½ orange

- 1½ cups cold water

- ¼ tsp pink salt

- Stevia or monk fruit to taste

Instructions:

Mix all ingredients and shake well. Sip chilled. Excellent for kidney support and fluid balance without sugar spikes.

Beet-Coconut Rehydration Juice

Ingredients:

- ½ cooked beet, chopped

- 1 cup coconut water

- Juice of ½ lemon

- 1 tbsp chia seeds

- Pinch of sea salt

Instructions:

Blend all ingredients, let chia soak for 10 minutes, then drink. Beets support nitric oxide production and blood pressure regulation.

Chapter 8

Batch Cooking and Meal Prep Made Simple

Make-Ahead Zepbound Breakfasts

Egg Muffin Cups with Veggies and Turkey

Ingredients:

- 8 eggs

- ½ cup chopped spinach

- ½ cup chopped bell peppers

- ¼ cup chopped onions

- ½ cup cooked ground turkey

- Salt and pepper to taste

- 1 tbsp olive oil

Instructions:

Preheat oven to 350°F. Grease a muffin tin with olive oil. Whisk eggs in a large bowl. Stir in veggies and turkey.

Pour into muffin cups and bake for 20–25 minutes. Store in fridge for up to 5 days.

Overnight Chia-Flax Pudding with Berries

Ingredients:

- ¼ cup chia seeds

- 1 tbsp ground flaxseed

- 1 cup unsweetened almond milk

- ½ tsp vanilla extract

- ½ cup fresh or frozen berries

- Stevia or monk fruit to taste

Instructions:

Mix chia, flax, milk, and vanilla in a jar. Stir well. Let sit 5 minutes, stir again, then refrigerate overnight. Top with berries in the morning.

Zucchini-Oat Protein Breakfast Bake

Ingredients:

- 2 cups rolled oats (gluten-free)

- 1 zucchini, shredded

- 2 eggs

- 1 scoop vanilla protein powder

- 1 tsp cinnamon

- ½ tsp baking powder

- 1 ½ cups almond milk

- Stevia to taste

Instructions:

Preheat oven to 350°F. Mix all ingredients in a bowl, then pour into a greased 8x8" baking dish. Bake 30–35 minutes. Slice into squares and refrigerate for grab-and-go breakfasts.

Avocado-Tahini Egg Salad Wraps

Ingredients:

- 6 boiled eggs, chopped

- 1 avocado

- 1 tbsp tahini

- 1 tsp mustard

- Salt, pepper, and paprika to taste

- Romaine leaves for wrapping

Instructions:

Mash avocado with tahini and mustard. Stir in chopped eggs and season. Scoop into romaine leaves. Store salad mix up to 3 days.

Pumpkin-Spice Protein Balls

Ingredients:

- ½ cup pumpkin purée

- 1 cup almond flour

- 1 scoop vanilla protein powder

- 1 tbsp ground flaxseed

- 1 tsp pumpkin pie spice

- Stevia to taste

Instructions:

Mix all ingredients. Roll into 1-inch balls. Refrigerate in an airtight container up to 5 days. Eat 2–3 for a quick fat-burning breakfast.

Almond Butter Zucchini Muffins (No Sugar)

Ingredients:

- 1 cup almond butter

- 1 zucchini, shredded and squeezed dry

- 2 eggs

- ½ tsp baking soda

- ½ tsp cinnamon

- 1 tsp vanilla extract

- Stevia or monk fruit

Instructions:

Mix all ingredients and scoop into muffin tins. Bake at 350°F for 18–20 minutes. Store in fridge for 5 days or freeze up to 1 month.

Prep-Ahead Lunches in Jars

Chicken Taco Salad Jar

Ingredients (per jar):

- ½ cup grilled chicken, chopped

- ¼ cup black beans

- ¼ cup corn (optional)

- ¼ cup chopped bell peppers

- ¼ avocado (sliced or mashed)

- 2 tbsp salsa

- 1 cup romaine lettuce

Instructions:

Layer salsa on bottom, followed by beans, corn, chicken, peppers, avocado, and lettuce last. Shake before eating.

Mediterranean Quinoa Jar

Ingredients (per jar):

- ½ cup cooked quinoa

- ¼ cup chopped cucumbers

118

- ¼ cup cherry tomatoes

- 2 tbsp hummus

- 1 tbsp olive oil + lemon juice

- 2 tbsp olives

- ¼ cup chickpeas

- ½ cup arugula or spinach

Instructions:

Layer quinoa first, followed by chickpeas, cucumbers, olives, tomatoes, dressing, hummus, and greens on top. Shake before serving.

Zepbound Tuna-Pesto Power Jar

Ingredients (per jar):

- 1 can tuna in water, drained

- 1 tbsp dairy-free pesto

- ½ cup spiralized zucchini

- ¼ cup shredded carrots

- ¼ avocado, sliced

- 1 cup spinach

- 1 tbsp lemon juice

Instructions:

Mix tuna with pesto and layer at the bottom. Add veggies in order, ending with spinach and lemon. Refrigerate up to 3 days.

Rainbow Veggie Jar with Tahini Dressing

Ingredients (per jar):

- ¼ cup shredded red cabbage

- ¼ cup shredded carrots

- ¼ cup chopped cucumbers

- ¼ cup chickpeas

- 2 tbsp tahini

- 1 tbsp apple cider vinegar

- 1 cup mixed greens

Instructions:

Mix tahini with vinegar and pour into jar. Layer cabbage, carrots, chickpeas, cucumbers, and greens. Shake to dress.

Lentil and Roasted Veggie Jar

Ingredients (per jar):

- ½ cup cooked lentils

- ¼ cup roasted sweet potatoes

- ¼ cup roasted zucchini

- 1 tbsp olive oil

- 1 tsp balsamic vinegar

- 1 cup baby kale

Instructions:

Layer oil and vinegar first, then lentils, sweet potatoes, zucchini, and kale last. Keeps in fridge 4–5 days.

Turkey and Cauliflower Rice Jar

Ingredients (per jar):

- ½ cup cooked ground turkey (seasoned with cumin and paprika)

- ½ cup cauliflower rice

- ¼ cup chopped red bell pepper

- ¼ cup chopped spinach

- 1 tbsp guacamole

- 1 tbsp lime juice

Instructions:

Add guacamole and lime juice to bottom. Layer cauliflower rice, turkey, peppers, and spinach. Shake to combine before eating.

Freezer-Friendly Dinners

Zucchini-Turkey Meatballs

Ingredients:

- 1 lb ground turkey

- 1 zucchini, grated and squeezed dry

- 1 egg

- 2 tbsp almond flour

- 1 tsp garlic powder

- 1 tsp Italian seasoning

- Salt and pepper

Instructions:

Mix ingredients. Roll into balls. Bake at 375°F for 20 minutes. Cool, then freeze in batches. Reheat and serve with cauliflower mash or zucchini noodles.

Cabbage Roll Casserole

Ingredients:

- 1 lb ground beef or turkey

- ½ onion, diced

- 2 cups chopped cabbage

- 1 cup diced tomatoes (no salt added)

- 1 tsp garlic powder

- 1 tsp smoked paprika

- Salt and pepper

Instructions:

Cook meat and onion, then add tomatoes and cabbage. Simmer 15–20 minutes. Cool and portion into containers. Freeze up to 2 months.

Broccoli-Cauliflower Bake with Chicken

Ingredients:

- 2 cups cooked shredded chicken

- 1 cup steamed broccoli

- 1 cup steamed cauliflower

- ¼ cup coconut cream

- 1 tsp garlic powder

- Salt and pepper

Instructions:

Mix everything and spread into a baking dish. Bake at 375°F for 20–25 minutes. Let cool and freeze. Reheat before serving.

Turkey Chili (No Beans)

Ingredients:

- 1 lb ground turkey

- 1 cup chopped zucchini

- ½ cup chopped bell peppers

- 1 cup crushed tomatoes

- 1 tsp cumin

- 1 tsp paprika

- ½ tsp cinnamon

- Salt and pepper

Instructions:

Cook turkey, add veggies and spices. Simmer 30 minutes. Cool and freeze in 1-cup portions. Serve alone or over cauliflower rice.

Stuffed Bell Peppers

Ingredients:

- 4 bell peppers, tops cut off and seeds removed

- 1 cup cooked ground beef or lentils

- ½ cup riced cauliflower

- ¼ cup diced tomatoes

- 1 tsp oregano

- Salt and pepper

Instructions:

Mix filling and stuff peppers. Bake at 375°F for 25–30 minutes. Cool and freeze individually.

Salmon Cakes with Dill

Ingredients:

- 1 can wild salmon, drained

- 1 egg

- 2 tbsp almond flour

- 1 tbsp chopped fresh dill

- ½ tsp garlic powder

- 1 tbsp lemon juice

Instructions:

Mix and form into patties. Bake or pan-fry until golden. Cool and freeze with parchment between each cake. Reheat and serve with sautéed greens.

Chapter 9

Dining Out While on Zepbound

How to Read Menus and Choose Wisely

Grilled Chicken Salad with Avocado and Olive Oil (Order Guide)

How to Order: Ask for grilled chicken breast over a bed of mixed greens, sliced avocado, cucumbers, cherry tomatoes, and red onions. Request olive oil and lemon on the side.

Swap: Skip croutons and sugary dressings. Add hard-boiled egg for protein boost.

Bunless Burger Plate with Roasted Veggies

How to Order: Ask for a lettuce-wrapped grass-fed beef or turkey burger. Add toppings like sautéed mushrooms, avocado, pickles, and mustard. Choose grilled or roasted veggies instead of fries.

Swap: No ketchup, no bun, no cheese sauce. Ask for extra greens instead.

Seared Salmon with Steamed Broccoli and Side Salad

How to Order: Choose grilled or pan-seared salmon without sauce. Add steamed broccoli and a small garden salad with vinaigrette.

Swap: Say no to rice or mashed potatoes. Double the non-starchy vegetables.

Chipotle Bowl Zepbound Style

How to Order: Base of greens and cauliflower rice, grilled chicken or steak, fajita veggies, pico de gallo, extra guacamole.

Swap: No beans, no rice, no cheese, no sour cream. Squeeze lime for flavor.

Asian Stir-Fry Without the Sugar

How to Order: Ask for steamed vegetables with grilled tofu, shrimp, or chicken. Request sauce on the side or choose garlic, ginger, or tamari only.

Swap: Replace noodles or rice with extra vegetables or ask for a side of shredded cabbage.

Mediterranean Plate with Clean Protein

How to Order: Grilled chicken or lamb skewers with cucumber-tomato salad, olives, and baba ghanoush.

Swap: Skip the pita. Ask for extra salad and grilled zucchini or eggplant instead.

Build-Your-Own Salad Bar Strategy

Recipe Format:

- Base: Spinach, kale, arugula

- Protein: Boiled eggs, grilled chicken, canned tuna, or smoked salmon

- Add-ins: Cucumber, tomatoes, artichoke hearts, olives, shredded carrots

- Fats: Avocado, seeds, olive oil

- Dressing: Olive oil, vinegar, lemon juice

Swap: No croutons, creamy dressings, dried fruit, or sweet vinaigrettes.

Fast-Food Egg Bites & Veggie Bowl Combo

How to Order: Choose egg bites made with whole eggs and cheese, pair with side of sautéed spinach or side salad if available.

Swap: Skip hash browns, bread, and orange juice. Opt for black coffee or herbal tea.

Zepbound Café Breakfast Plate

How to Order: 2 scrambled eggs or egg whites, avocado slices, grilled tomato, and sautéed greens or mushrooms.

Swap: Skip toast and breakfast potatoes. Add turkey sausage or smoked salmon if needed.

Best Restaurant Swaps

Zepbound Pizza Night Hack

How to Order: Choose gluten-free or cauliflower crust if available. Ask for light cheese or dairy-free, lots of veggies, grilled chicken or turkey, and tomato sauce without added sugar.

Swap: Avoid processed meats like pepperoni or sausage. Load up on arugula or spinach toppings post-bake.

Mexican Lettuce Tacos

How to Order: Grilled chicken, shrimp, or fish in lettuce wraps with avocado, cabbage slaw, and salsa.

Swap: Say no to tortillas, cheese, and sour cream. Add cilantro, lime, and jalapeños for flavor without carbs.

Zepbound Sushi Plate

How to Order: Order sashimi or naruto-style rolls (wrapped in cucumber instead of rice). Include seaweed salad and miso soup.

Swap: Avoid tempura, rice rolls, and sauces like eel sauce or spicy mayo.

Steakhouse Zepbound Plate

How to Order: Grass-fed steak, grilled asparagus or Brussels sprouts, side salad with olive oil.

Swap: No bread basket, mashed potatoes, or sugary sauces. Ask for grilled onions or mushrooms instead.

Indian Restaurant Clean Bowl

How to Order: Tandoori chicken or grilled paneer with sautéed spinach or cabbage, cucumber raita, and no naan or rice.

Swap: Avoid creamy curries (like tikka masala), fried samosas, or sweet chutneys.

Middle Eastern Falafel-Free Plate

How to Order: Grilled lamb or chicken kebab with tabbouleh (minimal bulgur), cucumber salad, and hummus.

Swap: Skip falafel, pita, and rice. Ask for more grilled eggplant or zucchini.

Thai Coconut Curry Bowl (No Sugar)

How to Order: Ask for green or red curry with chicken or shrimp, no sugar, served over steamed vegetables instead of rice.

Swap: Avoid noodle dishes and sweet sauces. Add extra Thai basil and lime.

Deli Roll-Ups

How to Order: Ask for nitrate-free turkey, lettuce, pickles, mustard, and tomato slices rolled together as wraps.

Swap: No bread, no mayonnaise-based salads. Ask for olives or hard-boiled eggs on the side.

Smoothie Bar Safe-Order

How to Order: Ask for spinach or kale base, ½ banana or berries, unsweetened almond milk, chia seeds, and unflavored protein powder.

Swap: Avoid agave, honey, sweetened protein powders, or fruit juice.

Greek Bowl No Grains

How to Order: Romaine lettuce base, grilled chicken or shrimp, olives, tomatoes, cucumbers, feta, and olive oil.

Swap: No rice, pita, or tzatziki with added sugar. Extra lemon for zing.

Zepbound Coffeehouse Snack

How to Order: Hard-boiled egg duo with unsweetened green tea or Americano. Add a packet of almonds if available.

Swap: No muffins, yogurt parfaits, or flavored lattes. Keep it simple, clean, and low-glycemic.

Tips for Social Events and Travel (Recipe-Style Solutions)

Potluck Cauliflower Rice Tabouli

Ingredients:

- 2 cups cauliflower rice (steamed and cooled)

- 1 cup chopped parsley

- ½ cup chopped cucumber

- ½ cup chopped tomato

- Juice of 1 lemon

- 2 tbsp olive oil

- Sea salt to taste

Instructions:

Mix everything and chill before serving. A refreshing side or main that travels well and supports satiety.

Travel Protein Trail Mix (Make Ahead)

Ingredients:

- ½ cup roasted almonds

- ½ cup pumpkin seeds

- ¼ cup coconut flakes

- 2 tbsp cacao nibs

- 1 tsp cinnamon

Instructions:

Mix all and store in a resealable bag. Perfect airport or road snack with blood sugar balance in mind.

On-the-Go Egg Muffins

Ingredients:

- 6 eggs

- ½ cup chopped spinach

- ¼ cup chopped bell peppers

- Sea salt and pepper

- Optional: nutritional yeast or feta

Instructions:

Whisk all, pour into muffin tins, bake at 350°F for 18–20 minutes. Pack for social gatherings or long drives.

Zepbound Travel Bento Box

Recipe:

- 2 hard-boiled eggs

- ½ avocado

- ¼ cup hummus

- Raw veggie sticks (cucumber, celery, bell pepper)

- 1 tbsp pumpkin seeds

Instructions:

Pack in a compartment container. Balanced fat, protein, and fiber on the go.

Mocktail Party Punch (No Sugar)

Ingredients:

- 1 cup sparkling water

- Juice of ½ lime

- Handful fresh mint

- Few sliced strawberries or cucumber slices

Instructions:

Stir and serve over ice. A clean option for events without derailing fat loss goals.

Portable Chia Jar

Ingredients:

- 3 tbsp chia seeds

- 1 cup unsweetened almond milk

- ½ tsp vanilla

- Berries or nuts for topping

Instructions:

Soak overnight. A grab-and-go breakfast or party dish that supports appetite control.

Cucumber-Wrapped Deli Rolls

Ingredients:

- Cucumber slices

- Nitrate-free turkey or chicken

- Mustard or avocado spread

Instructions:

Layer and roll. Secure with toothpicks for events or social snacking.

Pre-Party Fiber Smoothie Shot

Ingredients:

- ½ avocado

- 1 tbsp chia seeds

- 1 cup unsweetened almond milk

- Cinnamon to taste

Instructions:

Blend and drink before events to reduce cravings and stabilize energy.

Chapter 10

Special Diet Variations (Gluten-Free, Dairy-Free, Vegan-Friendly)

Zepbound Recipes for Food Sensitivities

Gluten-Free Cauliflower Power Bowl

Ingredients:

- 1 cup cauliflower rice
- ½ cup roasted chickpeas
- ½ avocado, sliced
- ¼ cup shredded carrots
- 2 tbsp tahini
- Juice of ½ lemon
- Sea salt to taste
- Fresh parsley for garnish

Instructions:

Steam cauliflower rice. Top with chickpeas, avocado, and carrots. Drizzle with tahini-lemon blend and garnish with parsley.

Dairy-Free Creamy Broccoli Soup

Ingredients:

- 1 tbsp olive oil

- 1 small onion, diced

- 2 garlic cloves, minced

- 3 cups chopped broccoli

- 2 cups vegetable broth

- ½ cup canned coconut milk

- Salt and pepper to taste

Instructions:

Sauté onion and garlic. Add broccoli and broth. Simmer 15 minutes, then blend with coconut milk until creamy.

Vegan Zucchini Noodle Stir-Fry

Ingredients:

- 2 medium zucchinis, spiralized

- 1 cup bell peppers, sliced

- ½ cup snap peas

- 2 tbsp coconut aminos

- 1 tsp sesame oil

- 1 tbsp toasted sesame seeds

- ½ tsp grated ginger

Instructions:

Stir-fry all veggies in sesame oil for 5 minutes. Add coconut aminos and ginger. Top with sesame seeds.

Allergy-Friendly Lentil Patties

Ingredients:

- 1 cup cooked lentils

- ¼ cup oat flour (gluten-free)

- 1 tbsp flaxseed meal + 3 tbsp water

- 1 tsp cumin

- 1 tbsp chopped fresh cilantro

- Salt to taste

Instructions:

Mix ingredients, form into patties. Bake at 375°F for 20 minutes or pan-fry in avocado oil until crisp.

Grain-Free Flatbread Wraps

Ingredients:

- ½ cup almond flour

- 2 tbsp ground flaxseed

- ¼ cup water

- ½ tsp garlic powder

- Pinch of salt

Instructions:

Mix ingredients into dough. Roll out into flat rounds. Cook on skillet 2–3 minutes each side.

Low-Allergen Berry Chia Pudding

Ingredients:

- 1 cup unsweetened almond or hemp milk

- ¼ cup chia seeds

- ½ cup mixed berries

- ½ tsp vanilla

- Stevia to taste

Instructions:

Stir all ingredients and refrigerate overnight. Serve chilled with extra berries on top.

Nightshade-Free Sweet Potato Hash

Ingredients:

- 1 cup diced sweet potato

- ¼ cup chopped zucchini

- ¼ cup chopped kale

- 1 tbsp olive oil

- 1 tsp turmeric

- Salt and pepper to taste

Instructions:

Sauté all ingredients in olive oil until potatoes are soft and edges crisp. Sprinkle turmeric and mix.

Egg-Free Protein Pancakes

Ingredients:

- ½ cup oat flour

- 1 scoop plant-based vanilla protein

- 1 tbsp flaxseed meal + 3 tbsp water

- ½ tsp baking powder

- ½ cup almond milk

- Coconut oil for cooking

Instructions:

Mix batter. Cook pancakes over medium heat for 2–3 minutes per side.

Plant-Based Protein Options

Smoky Tempeh Lettuce Boats

Ingredients:

- ½ block tempeh, sliced thin
- 1 tbsp coconut aminos
- ½ tsp smoked paprika
- Butter lettuce leaves
- Sliced cucumbers and avocado

Instructions:

Pan-fry tempeh with coconut aminos and paprika. Serve in lettuce wraps with fresh toppings.

Vegan Protein "Tuna" Salad

Ingredients:

- 1 can chickpeas, mashed
- 2 tbsp tahini
- 1 tbsp lemon juice
- 1 tbsp chopped celery

- 1 tbsp chopped pickles

- Salt, pepper, and dill to taste

Instructions:

Mix all ingredients and serve on gluten-free crackers or lettuce leaves.

Green Pea and Hemp Protein Soup

Ingredients:

- 1 tbsp olive oil

- 2 cups green peas

- 1 small onion, chopped

- 2 cups veggie broth

- 2 tbsp hemp seeds

- Salt and garlic to taste

Instructions:

Cook onion, add peas and broth, simmer 10 minutes. Blend with hemp seeds and serve warm.

Tofu Veggie Skewers

Ingredients:

- 1 block extra-firm tofu, cubed

- 1 zucchini, sliced

- 1 red onion, cut in chunks

- 2 tbsp olive oil

- 1 tbsp lemon juice

- 1 tsp oregano

Instructions:

Toss all ingredients. Skewer and grill or bake at 400°F for 20 minutes.

Crispy Chickpea Salad Bowl

Ingredients:

- 1 cup roasted chickpeas

- 2 cups mixed greens

- ½ cucumber, chopped

- 1 tbsp tahini

- Juice of ½ lemon

- Pinch of cumin

Instructions:

Assemble bowl with greens and veggies. Add chickpeas and drizzle with lemon-tahini dressing.

High-Protein Vegan Smoothie

Ingredients:

- 1 scoop plant-based protein powder

- 1 tbsp peanut butter

- 1 banana

- 1 tbsp ground flaxseed

- 1 cup almond milk

Instructions:

Blend until creamy. This smoothie provides lasting fullness and muscle-supporting plant protein.

Red Lentil Veggie Stew

Ingredients:

- 1 cup red lentils

- 2 cups chopped veggies (carrot, celery, zucchini)

- 1 tsp turmeric

- 1 tbsp olive oil

- 3 cups vegetable broth

- Salt and pepper

Instructions:

Sauté veggies. Add lentils, broth, and spices. Simmer 20 minutes until thick.

Simple Substitutions for Allergies

Nut-Free Sunflower Energy Bites

Ingredients:

- 1 cup sunflower seed butter

- ½ cup rolled oats (gluten-free)

- 1 tbsp chia seeds

- 1 tbsp maple syrup

- ½ tsp cinnamon

Instructions:

Mix, roll into balls, and chill. Perfect snack for nut-free, dairy-free diets.

Coconut Milk "Cheesy" Sauce

Ingredients:

- ½ cup canned coconut milk

- 2 tbsp nutritional yeast

- ½ tsp garlic powder

- Pinch turmeric

- Sea salt

Instructions:

Warm all ingredients in a saucepan. Stir until thick. Great dairy-free topping for veggies or pasta.

Egg-Free Breakfast Scramble

Ingredients:

- ½ block crumbled tofu

- ¼ cup chopped bell peppers

- ¼ cup spinach

- ½ tsp turmeric

- 1 tsp olive oil

- Salt and pepper

Instructions:

Sauté everything for 5–7 minutes. A high-protein, allergy-friendly breakfast option.

Gluten-Free Zucchini Lasagna

Ingredients:

- 2 zucchinis, thinly sliced lengthwise

- 1 cup marinara (no added sugar)

- 1 cup dairy-free ricotta (almond-based or cashew)

- Fresh basil

Instructions:

Layer zucchini slices, marinara, and dairy-free cheese. Bake at 375°F for 25 minutes.

Dairy-Free Cashew Cream Dressing

Ingredients:

- ½ cup soaked cashews

- 1 tbsp lemon juice

- ½ tsp garlic

- ¼ cup water

- Salt to taste

Instructions:

Blend until smooth. Use as salad dressing or veggie dip.

Oat-Free Grain Bowl

Ingredients:

- 1 cup cooked quinoa

- ½ cup steamed broccoli

- ¼ cup shredded carrot

- 1 tbsp tahini

- 1 tbsp lemon juice

- Salt and cumin

Instructions:

Mix all ingredients for an oat-free, gluten-free, allergen-friendly power bowl.

Soy-Free Vegan Protein Bowl

Ingredients:

- 1 cup cooked lentils

- ½ cup roasted sweet potato

- 1 tbsp hemp seeds

- 2 cups spinach

- 1 tbsp olive oil

- 1 tbsp balsamic vinegar

Instructions:

Toss and serve warm or chilled. Allergen-free and Zepbound-compatible.

Nut-Free Coconut Chia Yogurt Parfait

Ingredients:

- 1 cup plain coconut yogurt

- ¼ cup chia seeds

- ½ cup fresh berries

- Dash of cinnamon

Instructions:

Layer yogurt, chia, and berries. Let chill 10–15 minutes before eating.

Banana-Free Green Smoothie

Ingredients:

- 1 cup spinach

- ½ avocado

- ½ cucumber

- 1 scoop plant-based protein

- 1 cup almond milk

- Ice cubes

Instructions:

Blend smooth. Great for those avoiding bananas and sugar spikes.

Dairy-Free Chocolate Pudding

Ingredients:

- 1 ripe avocado

- 2 tbsp raw cacao powder

- 1 tbsp maple syrup or monk fruit

- 1 tsp vanilla extract

- Pinch sea salt

Instructions:

Blend until creamy. Chill and enjoy with a few fresh berries on top.

Chapter 11

Sweet Fixes Without the Sugar Crash

Low-Glycemic Desserts

Chia Seed Chocolate Pudding

Ingredients:

- 3 tbsp chia seeds

- 1 cup unsweetened almond milk

- 2 tbsp unsweetened cocoa powder

- 1 tsp vanilla extract

- 1-2 tsp monk fruit sweetener or stevia (adjust to taste)

Instructions:

1. Whisk almond milk, cocoa powder, vanilla, and sweetener in a bowl until smooth.

2. Stir in chia seeds.

3. Cover and refrigerate at least 4 hours or overnight until pudding thickens.

4.   Serve chilled with fresh raspberries or a sprinkle of cacao nibs.

Avocado Lime Mousse

Ingredients:

- 1 ripe avocado

- Juice and zest of 1 lime

- 2 tbsp unsweetened shredded coconut

- 1-2 tsp erythritol or monk fruit sweetener

- ½ tsp vanilla extract

Instructions:

1.   Blend avocado, lime juice, zest, sweetener, and vanilla until silky smooth.

2.   Spoon into small dishes and chill for 30 minutes.

3.   Garnish with toasted coconut flakes before serving.

Cinnamon-Spiced Pumpkin Custard

Ingredients:

- 1 cup pumpkin purée (unsweetened)

- 2 eggs

- ½ cup unsweetened almond milk

- 2 tbsp erythritol or other low-glycemic sweetener

- 1 tsp cinnamon

- ½ tsp nutmeg

- ½ tsp vanilla extract

Instructions:

1. Preheat oven to 350°F (175°C).

2. Whisk eggs, almond milk, and sweetener until smooth.

3. Stir in pumpkin, spices, and vanilla.

4. Pour mixture into ramekins.

5. Bake for 25-30 minutes until custard sets.

6.   Cool and serve chilled or warm.

Berry Coconut Cream Parfait

Ingredients:

•   1 cup mixed berries (blueberries, raspberries, strawberries)

•   1 cup coconut cream (chilled)

•   1 tbsp erythritol or monk fruit sweetener

•   1 tsp vanilla extract

•   2 tbsp unsweetened shredded coconut

Instructions:

1.   Whip coconut cream, sweetener, and vanilla until light and fluffy.

2.   Layer berries and coconut cream in serving glasses.

3.   Sprinkle shredded coconut on top.

4.   Serve immediately or chill for 1 hour.

Lemon-Blueberry Chia Tart

Ingredients for crust:

- 1 cup almond flour

- 2 tbsp coconut oil, melted

- 1 tbsp erythritol

- Pinch salt

Ingredients for filling:

- ½ cup lemon juice (freshly squeezed)

- 1 tbsp lemon zest

- ½ cup coconut cream

- 2 tbsp chia seeds

- 2 tbsp erythritol

- ½ cup fresh blueberries

Instructions:

1. Mix crust ingredients, press into tart pan. Bake at 350°F for 10 minutes. Let cool.

2.   Whisk filling ingredients, pour into cooled crust.

3.   Refrigerate at least 2 hours until set.

4.   Top with fresh blueberries before serving.

Fruit-Based Treats

Baked Cinnamon Apples

Ingredients:

- 2 medium apples, cored and sliced

- 1 tsp cinnamon

- 1 tbsp chopped walnuts

- 1 tsp coconut oil

- 1 tbsp erythritol or monk fruit sweetener

Instructions:

1.   Preheat oven to 375°F (190°C).

2.   Toss apples with cinnamon, sweetener, and coconut oil.

3.   Place in a baking dish, sprinkle walnuts on top.

4.   Bake for 25 minutes or until tender.

5.   Serve warm, optionally with a dollop of coconut yogurt.

Frozen Banana Bites with Dark Chocolate

Ingredients:

- 2 ripe bananas, sliced

- ½ cup 85% dark chocolate chips (sugar-free if possible)

- 1 tbsp coconut oil

- 1 tbsp crushed nuts or shredded coconut (optional)

Instructions:

1.   Freeze banana slices on a tray for 1 hour.

2.   Melt chocolate and coconut oil together.

3.   Dip frozen banana slices in melted chocolate, sprinkle nuts or coconut on top.

4.   Place on parchment paper and freeze until firm.

5.   Store in freezer, enjoy as cold bites.

Grilled Peaches with Almond Butter Drizzle

Ingredients:

- 2 ripe peaches, halved and pitted

- 2 tbsp almond butter

- 1 tsp lemon juice

- 1 tsp erythritol or sweetener of choice

Instructions:

1.   Preheat grill or grill pan.

2.   Grill peach halves cut-side down for 3-4 minutes until grill marks form.

3.   Warm almond butter slightly and mix with lemon juice and sweetener.

4.   Drizzle over grilled peaches and serve immediately.

Berry Salad with Mint and Lime

Ingredients:

- 1 cup mixed berries

- 1 tbsp fresh mint, chopped

- Juice of 1 lime

- 1 tsp erythritol or stevia

Instructions:

1. Toss berries with lime juice, sweetener, and mint.

2. Chill for 10 minutes before serving.

3. Perfect as a light, refreshing fruit dessert.

Baked Goods with Smart Sweeteners

Almond Flour Blueberry Muffins

Ingredients:

- 2 cups almond flour

- 1 tsp baking powder

- ¼ tsp salt

- 3 eggs

- ½ cup unsweetened almond milk

- ¼ cup erythritol or monk fruit sweetener

- 1 tsp vanilla extract

- 1 cup fresh or frozen blueberries

Instructions:

1.   Preheat oven to 350°F (175°C).

2.   Mix dry ingredients in a bowl.

3.   In another bowl, whisk eggs, almond milk, sweetener, and vanilla.

4.   Combine wet and dry ingredients, fold in blueberries gently.

5.   Spoon batter into muffin tins lined with paper cups.

6.   Bake 20-25 minutes until golden and a toothpick comes out clean.

7.   Cool completely before serving.

Coconut Flour Chocolate Chip Cookies

Ingredients:

- ½ cup coconut flour

- ¼ tsp baking soda

- Pinch salt

- 3 eggs

- ⅓ cup coconut oil, melted

- ¼ cup erythritol or preferred sweetener

- 1 tsp vanilla extract

- ½ cup sugar-free dark chocolate chips

Instructions:

1. Preheat oven to 350°F (175°C).

2. Mix coconut flour, baking soda, and salt.

3. Whisk eggs, coconut oil, sweetener, and vanilla.

4. Combine wet and dry ingredients, stir in chocolate chips.

5.   Drop tablespoon-sized scoops onto parchment-lined baking sheet.

6.   Bake 10-12 minutes until edges are golden.

7.   Cool before transferring to a wire rack.

Zucchini Bread with Walnuts

Ingredients:

- 1½ cups almond flour

- ½ cup shredded zucchini (squeezed dry)

- 3 eggs

- ¼ cup erythritol

- 1 tsp baking powder

- ½ tsp cinnamon

- ¼ cup chopped walnuts

- 1 tsp vanilla extract

Instructions:

1.   Preheat oven to 350°F (175°C).

2.   Combine almond flour, baking powder, cinnamon in a bowl.

3.   In a separate bowl, beat eggs, sweetener, vanilla.

4.   Stir wet ingredients into dry, fold in zucchini and walnuts.

5.   Pour into greased loaf pan.

6.   Bake 35-40 minutes or until toothpick inserted comes out clean.

7.   Cool completely before slicing.

Pumpkin Spice Energy Balls

Ingredients:

- 1 cup almond flour

- ½ cup pumpkin purée

- 2 tbsp chia seeds

- 2 tbsp erythritol or monk fruit sweetener

- 1 tsp pumpkin pie spice

- 1 tsp vanilla extract

Instructions:

1. Mix all ingredients in a bowl until sticky dough forms.

2. Roll into 1-inch balls.

3. Refrigerate for 1 hour before serving.

4. Store in fridge up to 5 days.

No-Bake Coconut Date Bars

Ingredients:

- 1 cup unsweetened shredded coconut

- 1 cup pitted Medjool dates

- ½ cup almond flour

- 2 tbsp coconut oil

- 1 tsp vanilla extract

- Pinch salt

Instructions:

1. Pulse dates and coconut in food processor until finely chopped.

2.   Add almond flour, coconut oil, vanilla, salt and pulse to combine.

3.   Press mixture into a lined 8x8-inch pan.

4.   Refrigerate for 2 hours until firm.

5.   Cut into bars and serve chilled.

Chapter 12

7-Day Zepbound Kickstart Meal Plan

Day 1

Breakfast: Green Fiber Smoothie

- 1 cup spinach

- ½ avocado

- 1 tbsp chia seeds

- 1 scoop vanilla protein

- 1 cup almond milk

- ½ frozen banana

Blend until smooth.

Lunch: Turkey Collard Wraps

- 2 collard green leaves

- 4 oz sliced turkey breast

- ¼ avocado, sliced

- 1 tbsp hummus

- Julienned cucumber and carrots

Wrap tightly.

Dinner: Zucchini Noodle Pesto Bowl

- 2 cups zucchini noodles

- 1 tbsp olive oil

- 3 oz grilled chicken

- 2 tbsp dairy-free pesto

Toss together and heat.

Snack: Cucumber Slices + Guacamole

- 1 cup cucumber slices

- ¼ cup fresh guacamole

Day 2

Breakfast: Cinnamon Coconut Protein Shake

- 1 scoop vanilla protein

- 1 tbsp shredded coconut

- ½ tsp cinnamon

- 1 cup almond milk

- ½ cup ice

Blend well.

Lunch: Egg and Spinach Salad

- 2 boiled eggs

- 2 cups spinach

- 1 tbsp olive oil

- 1 tbsp apple cider vinegar

- Sliced radish and avocado

Dinner: Baked Salmon with Asparagus

- 4 oz wild salmon

- 1 tsp olive oil

- Garlic powder, sea salt

- 1 cup asparagus

Bake at 375°F for 15 minutes.

Snack: Almonds + Blueberries

- 10 raw almonds
- ½ cup fresh blueberries

Day 3

Breakfast: Cacao-Chia Smoothie

- 1 scoop chocolate protein
- 1 tbsp chia seeds
- ½ banana
- 1 tsp raw cacao
- 1 cup oat milk

Blend until creamy.

Lunch: Cauliflower Rice Stir-Fry

- 1 cup cauliflower rice
- ½ cup bell pepper strips
- ½ cup shredded cabbage
- 1 tbsp coconut aminos

- 2 oz diced tofu

Sauté all for 6–8 minutes.

Dinner: Turkey Zucchini Boats

- 1 zucchini, halved

- 4 oz ground turkey

- 1 tbsp tomato paste

- Garlic, onion powder

Stuff and bake at 375°F for 15 minutes.

Snack: Celery Sticks + Almond Butter

- 2 celery stalks

- 1 tbsp unsweetened almond butter

Day 4

Breakfast: Blueberry Protein Smoothie

- ½ cup blueberries

- 1 scoop vanilla protein

- 1 tbsp hemp seeds

- 1 cup almond milk

- 1 tsp lemon zest

Blend until thick.

Lunch: Avocado Tuna Lettuce Boats

- ½ avocado

- 1 can tuna in water, drained

- 1 tbsp mustard

- Bibb lettuce leaves

Mash tuna with avocado and fill leaves.

Dinner: Chicken Fajita Bowl

- ½ grilled chicken breast

- ½ cup sautéed peppers and onions

- ½ cup cauliflower rice

- 1 tbsp guacamole

Assemble in a bowl.

Snack: Boiled Egg + Sliced Tomato

- 1 hard-boiled egg

- ½ tomato with salt and pepper

Day 5

Breakfast: Apple Pie Smoothie

- ½ apple

- 1 scoop vanilla protein

- 1 tsp cinnamon

- 1 tbsp flaxseed

- 1 cup almond milk

- Ice to taste

Blend thoroughly.

Lunch: Broccoli and Quinoa Bowl

- ½ cup cooked quinoa

- 1 cup steamed broccoli

- 1 tbsp tahini

- Juice of ½ lemon

Mix warm and serve.

Dinner: Shrimp and Veggie Stir-Fry

- 4 oz shrimp

- 1 cup zucchini and bell pepper

- 1 tbsp coconut aminos

- 1 tsp sesame oil

Stir-fry on high for 5 minutes.

Snack: Greek Yogurt + Berries (if tolerated)

- ½ cup plain Greek yogurt

- ¼ cup berries

Day 6

Breakfast: Avocado Matcha Smoothie

- ½ avocado

- ½ tsp matcha

- 1 scoop vanilla protein

- 1 cup almond milk

- 1 tbsp chia seeds

Blend until creamy.

Lunch: Chicken Collard Wrap

- 1 collard leaf

- 3 oz grilled chicken

- ¼ avocado

- 1 tbsp spicy mustard

- Julienned carrots

Roll tightly.

Dinner: Turkey Meatballs with Zoodles

- 4 turkey meatballs (baked)

- 1 cup zucchini noodles

- ¼ cup sugar-free marinara

Heat and serve warm.

Snack: Bell Pepper + Hummus

- ½ red bell pepper, sliced

- 2 tbsp hummus

Day 7

Breakfast: Raspberry Coconut Smoothie

- ½ cup raspberries

- 1 scoop protein

- 1 tbsp shredded coconut

- 1 cup almond milk

- 1 tbsp chia

Blend and chill.

Lunch: Egg and Avocado Bowl

- 2 boiled eggs, halved

- ½ avocado

- 1 tbsp olive oil

- Sea salt and pepper

Serve over arugula.

Dinner: Lemon Herb Chicken with Kale

- 4 oz chicken breast

- Juice of ½ lemon

- 1 tbsp olive oil

- 1 cup sautéed kale

Grill chicken and serve on kale.

Snack: Chia Pudding

- 2 tbsp chia seeds

- ½ cup almond milk

- 1 tsp cinnamon

- Stevia

Soak overnight.

Prep Tips and Time-Savers

- Hard-boil 6–8 eggs on Day 1 to use throughout the week.

- Grill 2–3 chicken breasts and store in glass containers.

• Chop veggies in advance (carrots, cucumbers, bell peppers).

• Make 2 smoothie bags for freezing: add fruit, greens, and seeds in bags for blending later.

• Batch cook cauliflower rice and quinoa and store in fridge.

• Make chia pudding in jars for easy grab-and-go snacks.

• Keep a jar of tahini dressing and hummus for quick bowl toppings and snacks.

Grocery List for the Week

Proteins

• Chicken breast (3)

• Ground turkey (8 oz)

• Canned tuna (1–2)

• Eggs (1 dozen)

• Shrimp (8 oz)

• Tofu (8 oz)

- Protein powder (plant-based or whey)

Vegetables

- Spinach (1 bunch)

- Kale (1 bunch)

- Zucchini (4)

- Bell peppers (2)

- Cucumber (2)

- Carrots (3)

- Cauliflower (1 head or riced)

- Avocados (4)

- Tomatoes (2)

- Lettuce/collard greens

- Asparagus

- Celery

Fruits

- Blueberries

- Raspberries

- Bananas (2)

- Green apples (2)

- Lemons (3)

- Lime (1)

- Frozen mixed berries

Pantry/Other

- Chia seeds

- Hemp seeds

- Flaxseed

- Olive oil

- Coconut aminos

- Apple cider vinegar

- Almond milk (2 cartons)

- Tahini

- Shredded coconut

- Almond butter

- Guacamole or ingredients to make it

- Hummus

- Tomato paste or sugar-free marinara

- Spices: cinnamon, cumin, garlic powder, onion powder, salt, pepper

Optional

- Matcha powder

- Raw cacao

- MCT oil

- Greek yogurt (if tolerated)

BONUS CHAPTER

Bonus 1: 250+ Smoothies & Juices for Zepbound Success

Weight Loss Smoothies

Coconut Matcha Burner

- 1 tsp matcha powder

- 1 cup unsweetened coconut milk

- ½ frozen avocado

- 1 scoop vanilla plant-based protein

- 1 tbsp MCT oil

- Stevia to taste

Blend until creamy and drink chilled.

Green Apple Cider Smoothie

- 1 green apple

- 1 tbsp apple cider vinegar

- 1 stalk celery

- Juice of ½ lemon

- ½ tsp cinnamon

- 1 cup water

- Ice cubes

Blend and serve immediately for a metabolic boost.

Peachy Fat-Burn Shake

- 1 cup frozen peaches

- 1 scoop vanilla protein powder

- 1 tbsp ground flaxseed

- ½ cup Greek yogurt (optional)

- 1 cup almond milk

- ½ tsp cinnamon

Blend and enjoy post-workout or as a meal.

Frozen Raspberry-Mint Smoothie

- 1 cup frozen raspberries

- Handful fresh mint

- ½ cucumber

- 1 tbsp chia seeds

- 1 cup water or coconut water

- Ice cubes

Blend until smooth and refreshing.

Lemon Basil Metabolism Smoothie

- Juice of 1 lemon

- 1 cup spinach

- ½ frozen banana

- ½ cup frozen pineapple

- 1 tbsp basil leaves

- 1 cup coconut water

Blend and enjoy bright citrus-herb flavor.

Zucchini-Cacao Smoothie

- ½ frozen zucchini

- 1 tbsp cacao powder

- 1 scoop protein powder

- ½ banana

- 1 cup almond milk

- Ice cubes

Blend until thick and creamy.

Berry-Chia Thermo Shake

- ½ cup mixed frozen berries

- 1 tbsp chia seeds

- 1 scoop collagen or plant-based protein

- ½ cup spinach

- 1 cup unsweetened almond milk

Blend and let sit 5 minutes to thicken.

Hormone-Balancing Juices

Beet & Carrot Estro-Tune Juice

- 1 small beet, peeled

- 2 carrots

- 1 apple

- ½ lemon

- 1-inch ginger

Juice all ingredients. Drink chilled to support estrogen detox pathways.

Cucumber-Dill Hormone Tonic

- 1 cucumber

- ½ lemon

- Handful dill

- 1 celery stalk

- ½ green apple

Juice and stir before serving. This fresh combo supports hormone regulation and hydration.

Grapefruit-Lime Thyroid Juice

- 1 grapefruit, peeled

- 1 lime

- ½ cup pineapple

- 1-inch fresh ginger

Juice and enjoy. Great for gentle liver support and thyroid-friendly nutrients.

Pineapple-Parsley Juice

- 1 cup pineapple
- 1 handful parsley
- 1 cucumber
- ½ lemon
- 1-inch turmeric root

Juice all ingredients. Anti-inflammatory and estrogen-balancing.

Zesty Celery-Ginger Juice

- 3 stalks celery
- 1 green apple
- 1-inch ginger
- ½ lemon
- Dash cayenne (optional)

Juice and serve over ice.

Berry-Lavender Adaptogen Juice

- ½ cup blueberries

- 1 tsp dried lavender flowers (steeped and cooled)

- ½ lemon

- 1 apple

- ½ cucumber

Juice and stir in cooled lavender tea. Balances stress hormones naturally.

Fennel-Pear Harmony Juice

- ½ fennel bulb

- 1 ripe pear

- 1 stalk celery

- ½ lemon

Juice and drink to support gut-hormone balance and calm inflammation.

Gut-Friendly, Anti-Inflammatory, and Detox Options

Turmeric Mango Smoothie

- ½ cup frozen mango

- 1 tsp turmeric powder

- Pinch of black pepper

- 1 tbsp chia seeds

- 1 scoop protein powder

- 1 cup coconut milk

Blend and serve cold for an anti-inflammatory kick.

Aloe-Green Gut Smoothie

- ½ cup aloe vera juice (food-grade)

- 1 cup spinach

- ½ cucumber

- 1 tbsp flaxseed

- ½ cup frozen papaya

- 1 cup water

Blend until smooth and silky.

Carrot-Ginger Detox Juice

- 2 carrots

- 1-inch ginger

- ½ apple

- ½ lemon

- 1 celery stalk

Juice and serve. Perfect for liver and gut health.

Papaya Mint Soother Smoothie

- ½ cup papaya

- 1 tbsp fresh mint

- 1 tbsp flaxseed

- ½ cup coconut water

- Ice cubes

Blend to reduce bloating and aid digestion.

Cabbage-Celery Juice

- ½ cup red cabbage

- 2 celery stalks

- 1 apple

- 1 lemon

Juice and drink immediately. Supports stomach lining and digestive repair.

Golden Pineapple Elixir

- 1 cup pineapple

- ½ inch turmeric

- 1 tbsp apple cider vinegar

- ½ lime

- ½ cup water

Juice or blend and strain if desired. Drink daily for inflammation reduction.

Parsley-Cilantro Cleansing Juice

- 1 cup parsley

- 1 cup cilantro

- 1 cucumber

- 1 green apple

- ½ lemon

Juice all ingredients. Best enjoyed fresh and cold.

Cranberry-Ginger Flush Smoothie

- ½ cup unsweetened cranberry juice

- 1 tbsp chia seeds

- ½ frozen banana

- 1 cup water

- 1-inch fresh ginger

Blend and let sit for 5 minutes before drinking.

Seasonal Flavor Rotations

Spring Smoothie Picks

Strawberry-Basil Cooler

- 1 cup strawberries

- 4 basil leaves

- ½ lemon

- 1 tbsp hemp seeds

- 1 cup coconut water

Blend and sip fresh.

Asparagus-Apple Green Smoothie

- 2 cooked asparagus stalks

- 1 green apple

- 1 cup spinach

- Juice of ½ lemon

- 1 cup water

Blend until fully smooth.

Pea-Pear Mint Shake

- ½ cup thawed frozen peas

- 1 pear

- 1 tbsp mint

- ½ cup Greek yogurt

- 1 cup almond milk

Blend until creamy and sweet.

Summer Smoothie Picks

Watermelon-Cucumber Refresher

- 1 cup watermelon

- ½ cucumber

- ½ lime

- Mint leaves

- Ice cubes

Blend and enjoy ice-cold.

Peach-Turmeric Smoothie

- 1 ripe peach

- ½ tsp turmeric

- 1 tbsp chia seeds

- 1 scoop vanilla protein

- 1 cup almond milk

Blend and chill.

Blueberry-Lavender Dream Shake

- ½ cup blueberries

- ½ tsp dried lavender (steeped)

- ½ banana

- 1 scoop collagen

- 1 cup almond milk

Blend and serve with lavender garnish.

Fall Smoothie Picks

Apple-Cinnamon Protein Shake

- 1 green apple

- 1 tsp cinnamon

- 1 scoop vanilla protein

- 1 tbsp ground flaxseed

- 1 cup oat milk

Blend and enjoy warm or cold.

Pumpkin-Ginger Smoothie

- ½ cup pumpkin purée

- 1 tbsp grated ginger

- 1 tsp pumpkin spice

- 1 scoop protein powder

- 1 cup almond milk

Blend and sprinkle with nutmeg.

Carrot-Pear Autumn Smoothie

- 1 small pear

- ½ cup shredded carrot

- 1 tbsp hemp seeds

- ½ tsp cinnamon

- 1 cup almond milk

Blend to smooth texture.

Winter Smoothie Picks

Clementine-Spinach Shake

- 2 clementines, peeled

- 1 cup spinach

- ½ banana

- 1 tbsp chia seeds

- 1 cup coconut milk

Blend and drink fresh.

Spiced Cranberry Detox Smoothie

- ½ cup unsweetened cranberry juice

- 1 tbsp ground flaxseed

- ½ tsp cinnamon

- 1 scoop vanilla protein

- 1 cup almond milk

Blend with ice.

Pineapple-Ginger Immunity Shake

- ½ cup pineapple

- 1-inch ginger

- ½ orange, peeled

- ½ cup water

- Ice cubes

Blend and drink to ward off inflammation and support immune balance.

Bonus 2: Weekly and Monthly Shopping Lists

WEEKLY SHOPPING LIST-BASED RECIPE PREP (Zepbound Edition)

Weekly Core Ingredients (repeatable all month):

• Leafy Greens: Spinach, Kale, Romaine, Arugula

• Cruciferous Veg: Broccoli, Cauliflower, Cabbage

• Low-Starch Veggies: Zucchini, Cucumber, Bell Pepper, Celery

• Lean Proteins: Chicken Breast, Salmon, Turkey, Eggs

• Plant-Based Proteins: Tempeh, Tofu, Lentils, Chickpeas

• Healthy Fats: Avocado, Chia Seeds, Hemp Seeds, Olive Oil, Almond Butter

• Fruits (Low-Glycemic): Berries, Green Apples, Lemons, Grapefruit

- Liquids: Coconut Water, Almond Milk, Bone Broth

- Spices & Seasonings: Ginger, Cinnamon, Turmeric, Garlic Powder

- Smoothie Add-ins: Protein Powder, Ground Flaxseed, MCT Oil

WEEK 1 MEAL PREP RECIPES

Grilled Chicken & Zucchini Bowls

Ingredients:

- 4 chicken breasts

- 2 zucchinis, sliced

- 1 red onion, quartered

- 2 tbsp olive oil

- 1 tsp Italian seasoning

- Salt and pepper

Instructions:

Toss chicken and veggies with olive oil and seasoning. Grill until cooked. Divide into 4 portions. Store with leafy greens for lunch bowls.

Avocado Egg Salad Lettuce Wraps

Ingredients:

- 4 hard-boiled eggs

- 1 ripe avocado

- 1 tbsp lemon juice

- ½ tsp garlic powder

- 1 tbsp chopped chives

- Romaine lettuce leaves

Instructions:

Mash eggs and avocado together with lemon, garlic, and chives. Spoon into lettuce leaves. Makes 3 servings.

Kale & Chickpea Stew (Slow Cooker)

Ingredients:

- 1 can chickpeas

- 2 cups kale

- 1 chopped onion

- 1 tbsp olive oil

- 3 cups veggie broth

- 1 tsp cumin

- Salt to taste

Instructions:

Combine ingredients in slow cooker. Cook on low for 6 hours. Yields 4 portions for lunch or dinner.

Berries & Chia Pudding Jars

Ingredients:

- 2 tbsp chia seeds per jar

- ½ cup unsweetened almond milk

- Handful mixed berries

- Dash cinnamon

Instructions:

Mix chia and milk in jars. Stir. Refrigerate overnight. Add berries in morning. Prepare 4 jars at once for snacks.

WEEK 2: SHOPPING LIST REPEATS + SWAPS

Swap:

- Zucchini for Cauliflower

- Chicken for Salmon

- Chia for Ground Flax

- Spinach for Arugula

- Blueberries for Strawberries

WEEK 2 MEAL PREP RECIPES

Cauliflower Rice Stir-Fry

Ingredients:

- 2 cups riced cauliflower

- ½ cup chopped bell peppers

- 1 egg

- 1 tbsp coconut aminos

- 1 tsp sesame oil

- Scallions for garnish

Instructions:

Sauté veggies in sesame oil. Add riced cauliflower. Scramble in egg. Pour in coconut aminos. Stir-fry 5 minutes.

Grilled Salmon with Cucumber Salsa

Ingredients:

- 2 salmon fillets

- 1 tbsp olive oil

- Juice of 1 lemon

- ½ cucumber, diced

- 1 tbsp red onion, minced

- 1 tbsp parsley

Instructions:

Grill salmon with olive oil and lemon. Mix salsa ingredients. Serve salsa over salmon. Meal-prep 2–3 portions.

Tempeh & Arugula Power Bowls

Ingredients:

- 1 block tempeh, cubed

- 2 cups arugula

- ½ avocado

- 1 tbsp tahini

- Juice of ½ lemon

- 1 tbsp water

Instructions:

Sear tempeh in skillet. Toss with arugula and sliced avocado. Whisk tahini, lemon, water into dressing. Drizzle and serve.

MONTHLY ROTATION RECIPES BY CATEGORY

BREAKFAST BATCH OPTIONS

Egg Muffin Cups (Freezer-Friendly)

Ingredients:

- 6 eggs

- ½ cup spinach

- ¼ cup chopped peppers

- ¼ cup diced onions

- Salt and pepper

Instructions:

Mix all ingredients. Pour into muffin tins. Bake 20 minutes at 350°F. Cool and freeze in bags. Reheat as needed.

Berry Protein Smoothie Packs

Ingredients (per pack):

- ½ cup frozen berries

- ½ banana

- 1 tbsp flaxseed

- 1 scoop protein powder

Instructions:

Store ingredients in freezer bags. Dump into blender with 1 cup almond milk for instant smoothies.

DINNER RECIPES

Stuffed Bell Peppers (Turkey Version)

Ingredients:

- 3 bell peppers

- 1 lb ground turkey

- ½ cup cauliflower rice

- 1 tsp Italian seasoning

- Salt and pepper

Instructions:

Cut peppers in half. Brown turkey. Mix with rice and seasoning. Fill peppers and bake at 375°F for 25 minutes.

Cabbage Stir-Fry with Tofu

Ingredients:

- 2 cups shredded cabbage

- ½ block firm tofu

- 1 tbsp sesame oil

- 1 tbsp coconut aminos

- Garlic, minced

Instructions:

Pan-fry tofu. Add garlic and cabbage. Stir-fry with oil and coconut aminos. Serve warm. Makes 3 servings.

PORTION CONTROL & FOOD JOURNAL TEMPLATE RECIPES

Portion Meal Prep Trays (Mix & Match Ideas)

Tray 1 – Lean Protein + Veg + Carb-Controlled

- 4 oz grilled chicken

- ½ cup roasted broccoli

- ½ cup mashed cauliflower

Tray 2 – Plant-Based Protein

- ½ cup lentils

- 1 cup arugula + shredded carrots

- 1 tbsp olive oil dressing

Tray 3 – Omega-Fat Focused

- 4 oz grilled salmon

- 1 cup sautéed spinach

- ¼ avocado

Tray 4 – Zepbound Snack Trays

- 1 boiled egg

- 1 tbsp almond butter

- ½ apple slices

Daily Smoothie Prep Journal Plan

Day 1:

- Spinach + avocado + lemon + chia + water

Day 2:

- Matcha + collagen + flax + almond milk

Day 3:

- Berries + hemp + protein powder + almond milk

Day 4:

- Cucumber + celery + parsley + lime

Repeat or rotate. Log hunger, fullness, and energy levels post-drink.

Made in United States
Orlando, FL
16 June 2025

62180813R00118